AVERY
Para ti mi niño
Con mucho amor
Feliz Cumpleaño
Te quiero amor
Tu abuela

PRESCHOOL SIGHT WORDS

FOR KIDS

Teach ME!

THIS BOOK BELONGS TO:

____

Teach ME! series design by Emanuelle Selman
Illustrations by Maryam Iqbal

Teach ME! Publishing Co., Ltd.
teachmeforkids.com

TABLE OF CONTENTS

JUST FOR YOU

A FREE GIFT TO OUR READERS

Download a free sample of our next activity or coloring book and start enjoying all the fun new activities we send your way today! Visit this link:

www.teachmeforkids.com

INTRODUCTION

It's nice to meet you! My name is Emanuelle Selman and I, along with my amazing team, create all of the books here at Teach ME!. I'm so glad you're enjoying one of our books and I can't wait for you to see all of the other books we have coming your way.

If you sign up for our mailing list, we send out free activities twice a week and you will always get a free sample of every new activity or coloring book that comes out. Our mailing list is meant for you to get free activities for your kids and for us to be able to share them with you.

At Teach ME!, all of our books follow the current curriculum. We have paired visual skills, printing skills, memory skills and more with all of the core concepts teachers focus on in the primary years. If it's in the curriculum, we have found a way to add it to our books.

Our hope is to be able to provide fun activities that help your child learn what they need to know in interactive and entertaining ways. Classes provide the structure but we provide the fun.

So jump in, have fun and get learning. We hope you love our books as much as we love making them. And we can't wait to share all that we have in store for your little ones.

Love always,
Emanuelle and Team

SAY & SPELL

a

Today we are going to learn the word 'a'. I'll read the word out loud and show you the direction the arrow goes with my finger. Then it will be your turn. Let's do this 3 times.

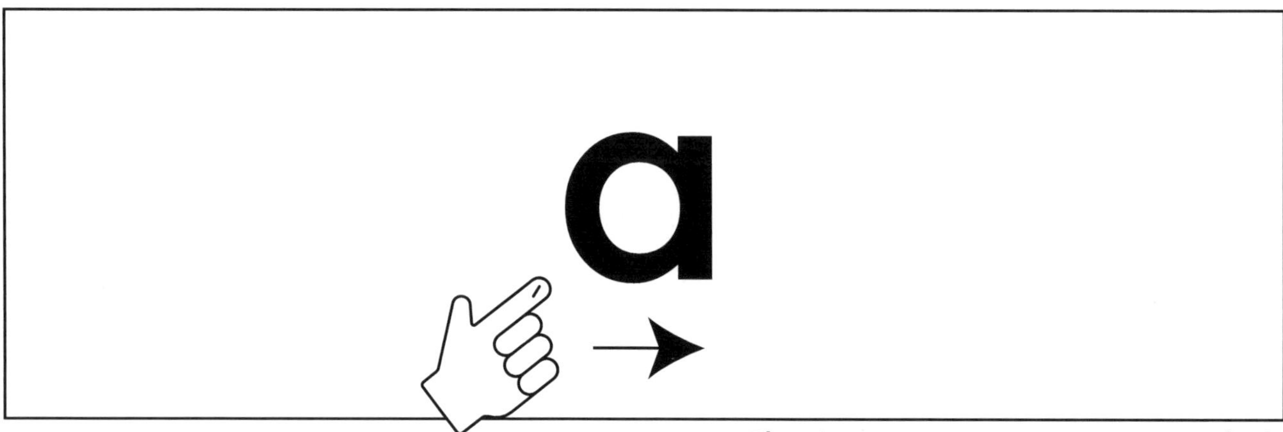

That's great! a. I am a great kid!

Now let's learn to SPELL our new word. Say the new word out loud again but this time, spell out the letters. Let's do this 3 times.

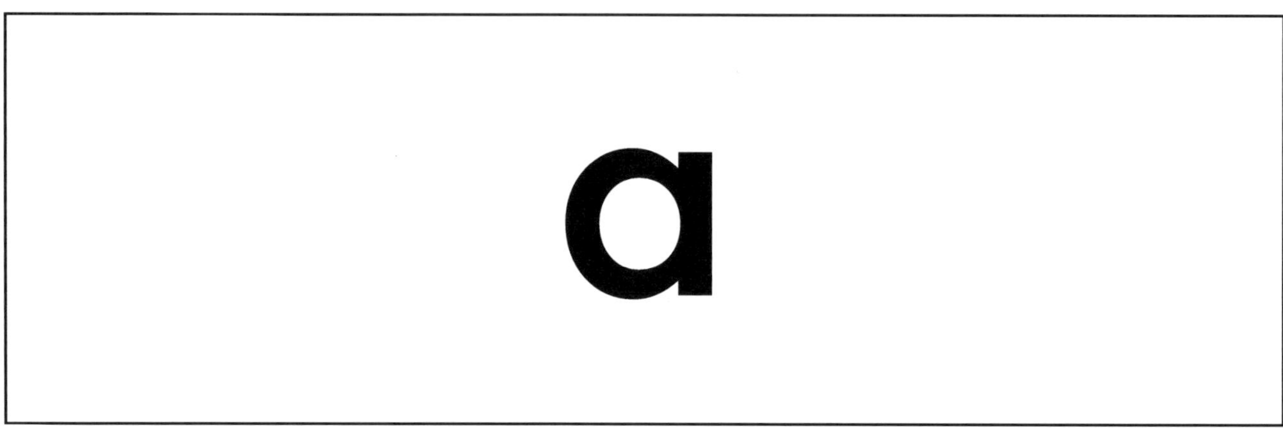

Fantastic!

Now that you can say and spell the word, let's practice tracing the letters. Using your pointer finger, trace each letter in the sky in front of you. Let's do this 3 times.

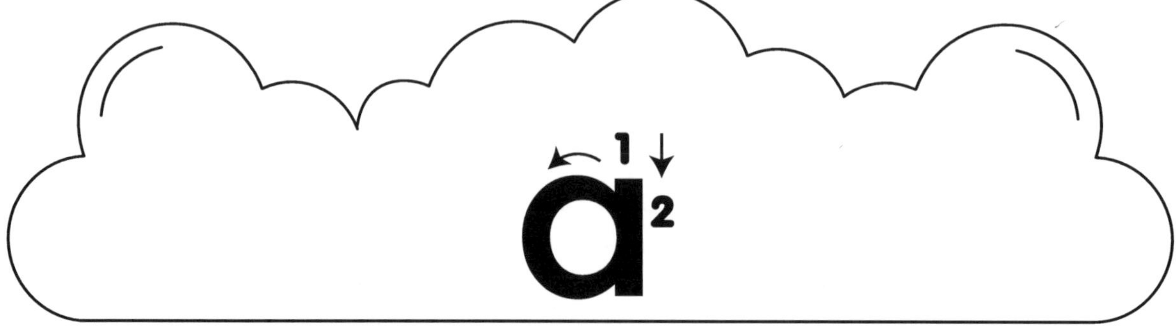

PRINT & RECOGNIZE

Now it's time to practice printing on paper. With your pencil, trace the dots and then practice on your own.

To really remember our new word, let's see if we can recognize the word among other words that look similar. Find all of the 'a' words below and draw a circle around them. Hint: There should be 6.

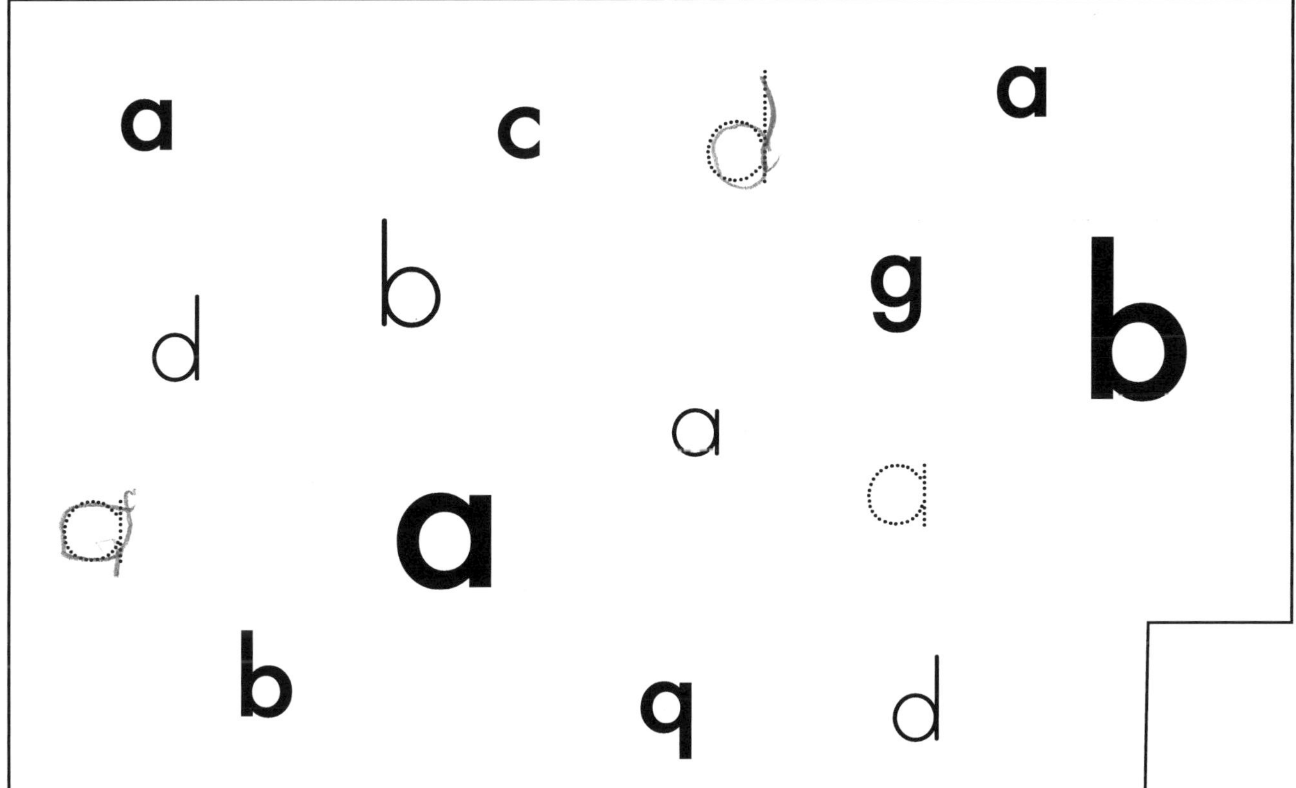

Amazing! Let's move on. The next word is and.

SAY & SPELL

and

Today we are going to learn the word 'and'. I'll read the word out loud and show you the direction the arrow goes with my finger. Then it will be your turn. Let's do this 3 times.

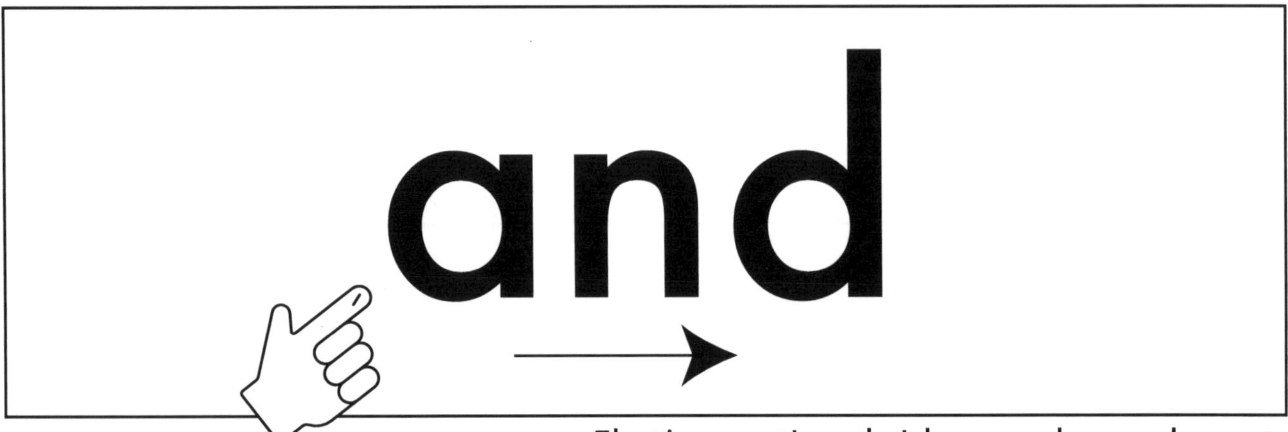

That's great! and. I have a dog and a cat.

Now let's learn to SPELL our new word. Say the new word out loud again but this time, spell out the letters. Let's do this 3 times.

Fantastic!

Now that you can say and spell the word, let's practice tracing the letters. Using your pointer finger, trace each letter in the sky in front of you. Let's do this 3 times.

PRINT & RECOGNIZE

Now it's time to practice printing on paper. With your pencil, trace the dots and then practice on your own.

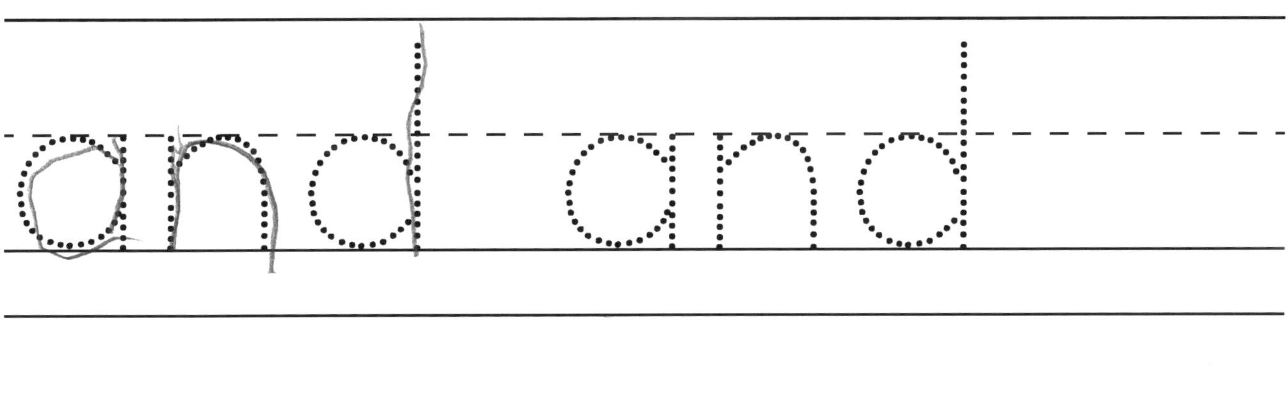

Let's see if we can recognize the words in the picture below. Color all of the bugs that have the word 'and' below them. Hint: There should be 3 bugs to color.

Amazing! Let's move on. The next word is away.

SAY & SPELL

The next word we are going to learn is 'away'. I'll read the word out loud and show you the direction the arrow goes with my finger. Then it will be your turn. Let's do this 3 times.

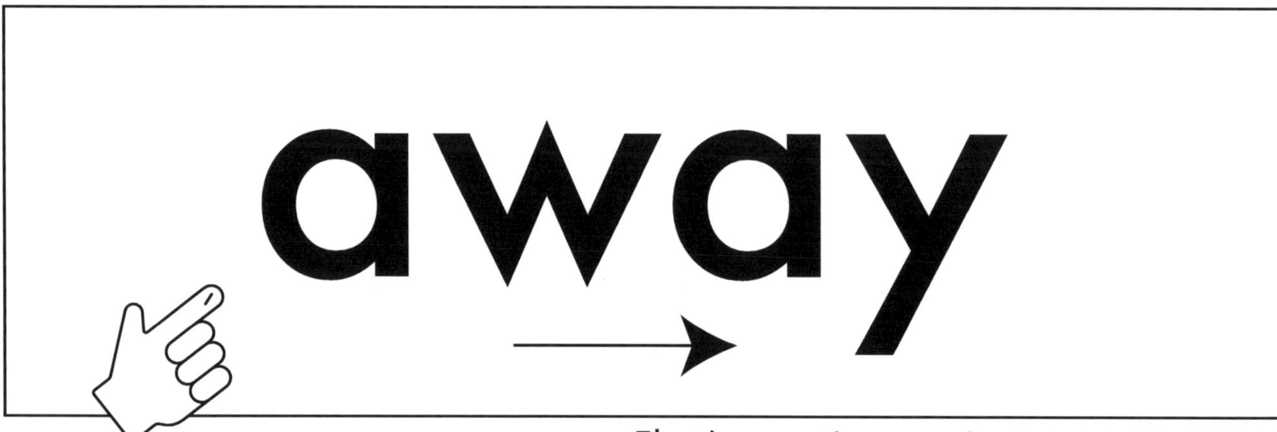

That's great! away. I put my toys away.

Now let's learn to SPELL our new word. Say the new word out loud again but this time, spell out the letters. Let's do this 3 times.

Fantastic!

Now that you can say and spell the word, let's practice tracing the letters. Using your pointer finger, trace each letter in the sky in front of you. Let's do this 3 times.

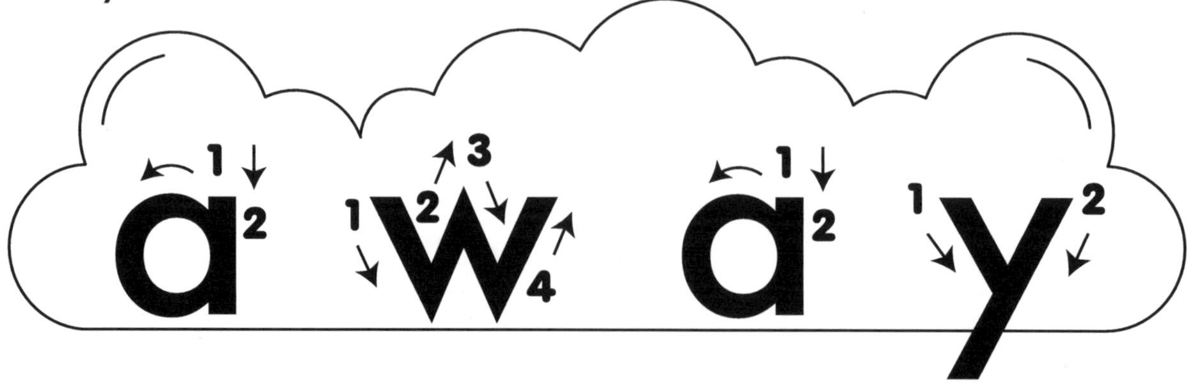

PRINT & RECOGNIZE

Now it's time to practice printing on paper. With your pencil, trace the dots and then practice on your own.

away away

Let's see if we can recognize the words in the picture below. Circle all of the stars that have the word 'away' in them. Then color them all in. Hint: There are 5 stars to color.

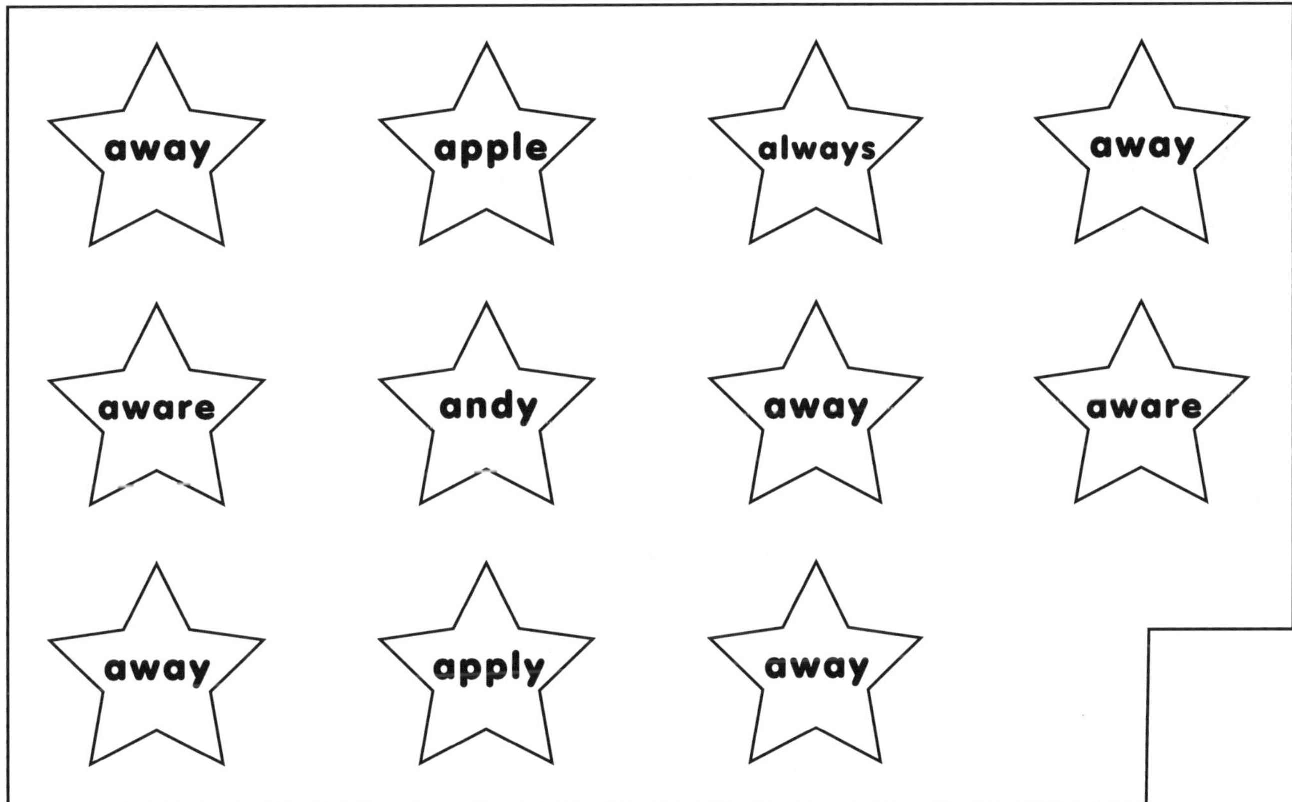

Amazing! Let's review and play a game.

FIND THE MATCHING WORD

Read the sentences below and find the matching word from the legend. The words are in the legend twice. Circle the missing word when you find it, say it out loud and write it in the space provided.

away	and	a	and	a	away

1. I am going ________ today.

2. First, I am getting on ______ plane.

3. Then, a boat ________ a train.

4. Finally, I check into ______ hotel.

5. ______ then, we go to Disneyland!

6. Ok goodbye! ________ we go!

CREATE YOUR OWN STORY

Each player makes up one line of the story and writes it down. Fold the page over or cover the line and the next player continues. Continue until the lines are complete and then read out your funny story. The words we are practicing are highlighted in bold so you can see how they fit into the story.

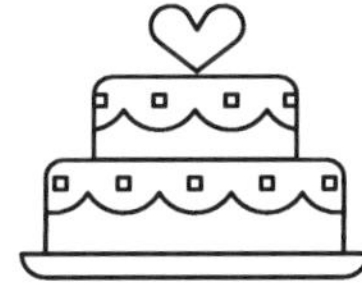

1. **A** friendly ______(animal)______,

2. Met **a** jolly ______(animal)______,

3. **And away** they went to ____(place)____,

4. Where the ___(#1)___ said ___(your choice)___,

5. **And** the ___(#2)___ said ___(your choice)___,

6. **And** they all flew **away** to the stars!

SAY & SPELL

Today we are going to learn the word 'big'. I'll read the word out loud and show you the direction the arrow goes with my finger. Then it will be your turn. Let's do this 3 times.

big

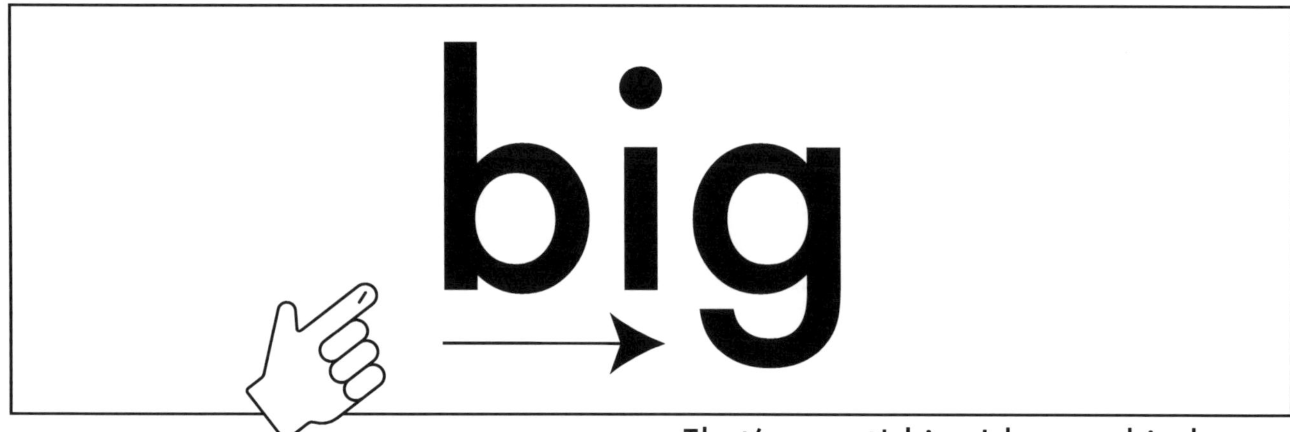

That's great! big. I have a big house.

Now let's learn to SPELL our new word. Say the new word out loud again but this time, spell out the letters. Let's do this 3 times.

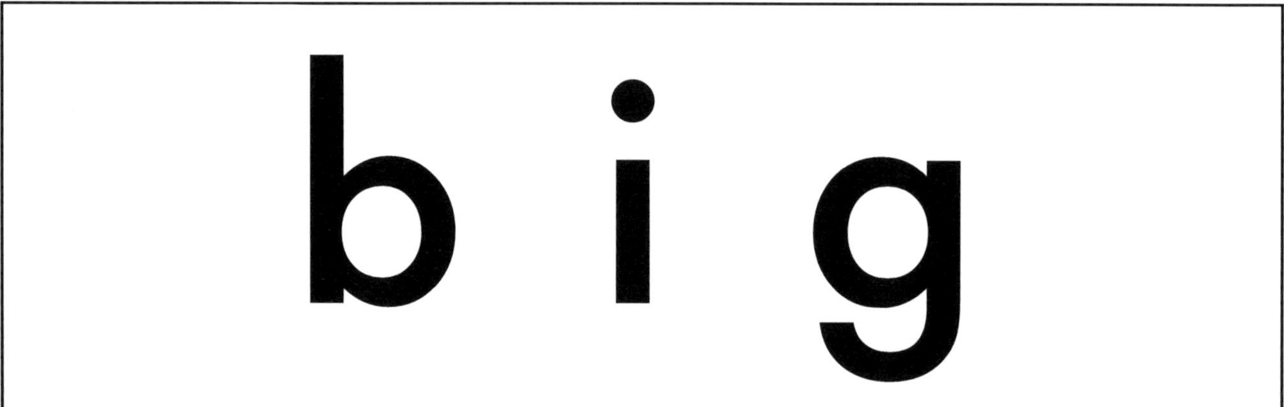

Fantastic!

Now that you can say and spell the word, let's practice tracing the letters. Using your pointer finger, trace each letter in the sky in front of you. Let's do this 3 times.

PRINT & RECOGNIZE

Now it's time to practice printing on paper. With your pencil, trace the dots and then practice on your own.

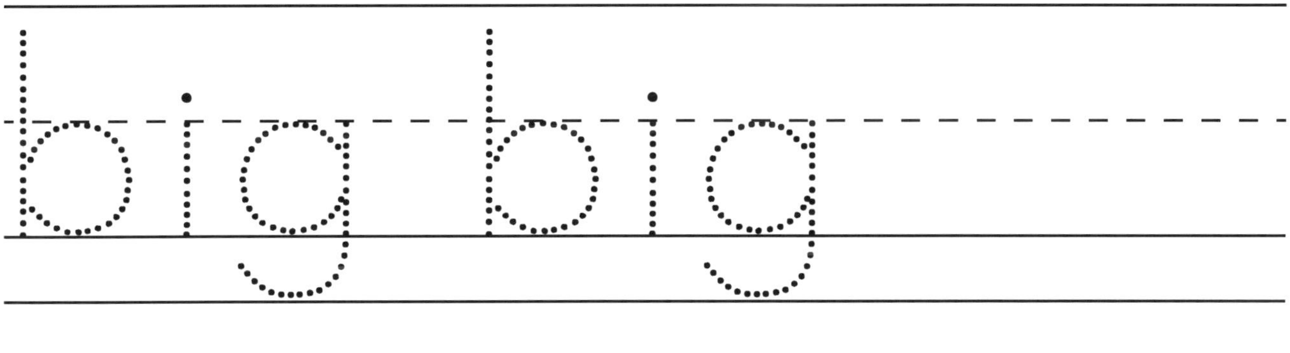

Let's see if we can recognize the words in the picture below. Find the word 'big' in the word search below and circle the letters. Hint: The word is in the search 4 times.

v	u	d	k	o	b	e
q	b	n	b	a	i	y
b	i	g	r	m	g	w
h	g	x	b	i	g	

Amazing! Let's move on. The next word is blue.

SAY & SPELL

blue

Today we are going to learn the word 'blue'. I'll read the word out loud and show you the direction the arrow goes with my finger. Then it will be your turn. Let's do this 3 times.

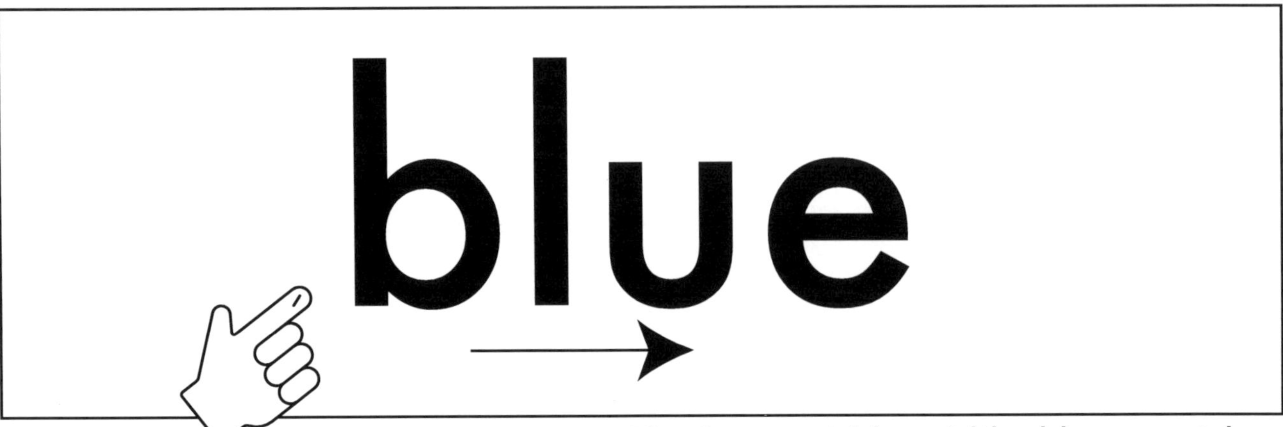

That's great! blue. I like blue popsicles.

Now let's learn to SPELL our new word. Say the new word out loud again but this time, spell out the letters. Let's do this 3 times.

b l u e

Fantastic!

Now that you can say and spell the word, let's practice tracing the letters. Using your pointer finger, trace each letter in the sky in front of you. Let's do this 3 times.

PRINT & RECOGNIZE

Now it's time to practice printing on paper. With your pencil, trace the dots and then practice on your own.

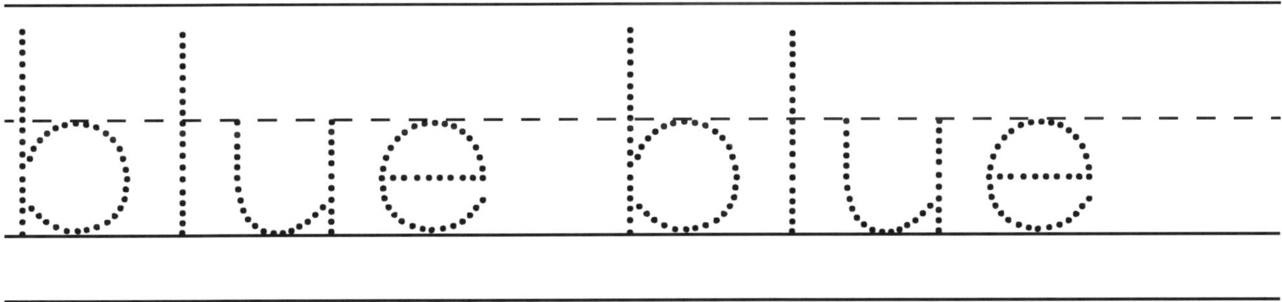

Let's figure out the image below by connecting all of the dots with the word 'blue'. Stay away from similar words as they will not help you complete the image. Hint: The image is great on hot days!

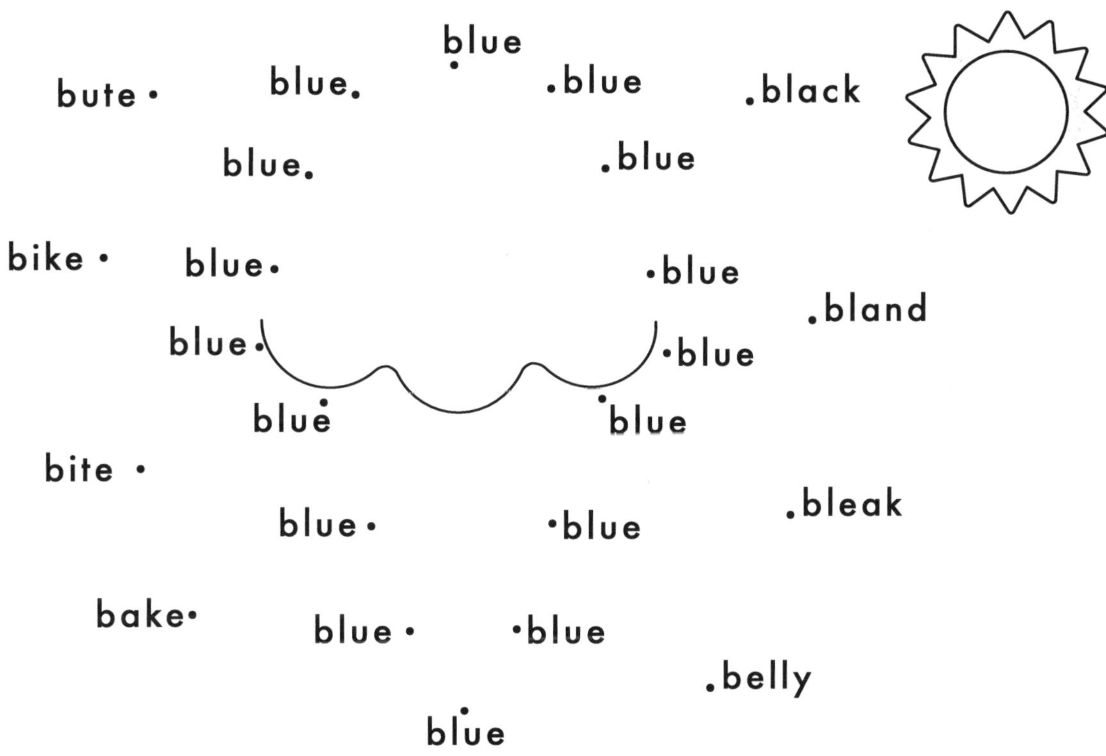

Amazing! Let's move on. The next word is can.

SAY & SPELL

can

Today we are going to learn the word 'can'. I'll read the word out loud and show you the direction the arrow goes with my finger. Then it will be your turn. Let's do this 3 times.

That's great! can. I can do it!

Now let's learn to SPELL our new word. Say the new word out loud again but this time, spell out the letters. Let's do this 3 times.

c a n

Fantastic!

Now that you can say and spell the word, let's practice tracing the letters. Using your pointer finger, trace each letter in the sky in front of you. Let's do this 3 times.

PRINT & RECOGNIZE

Now it's time to practice printing on paper. With your pencil, trace the dots and then practice on your own.

can can

Let's see if we can recognize the words in the picture below. Match all of the different ways the word 'can' can be written by drawing a line between pairs that match.

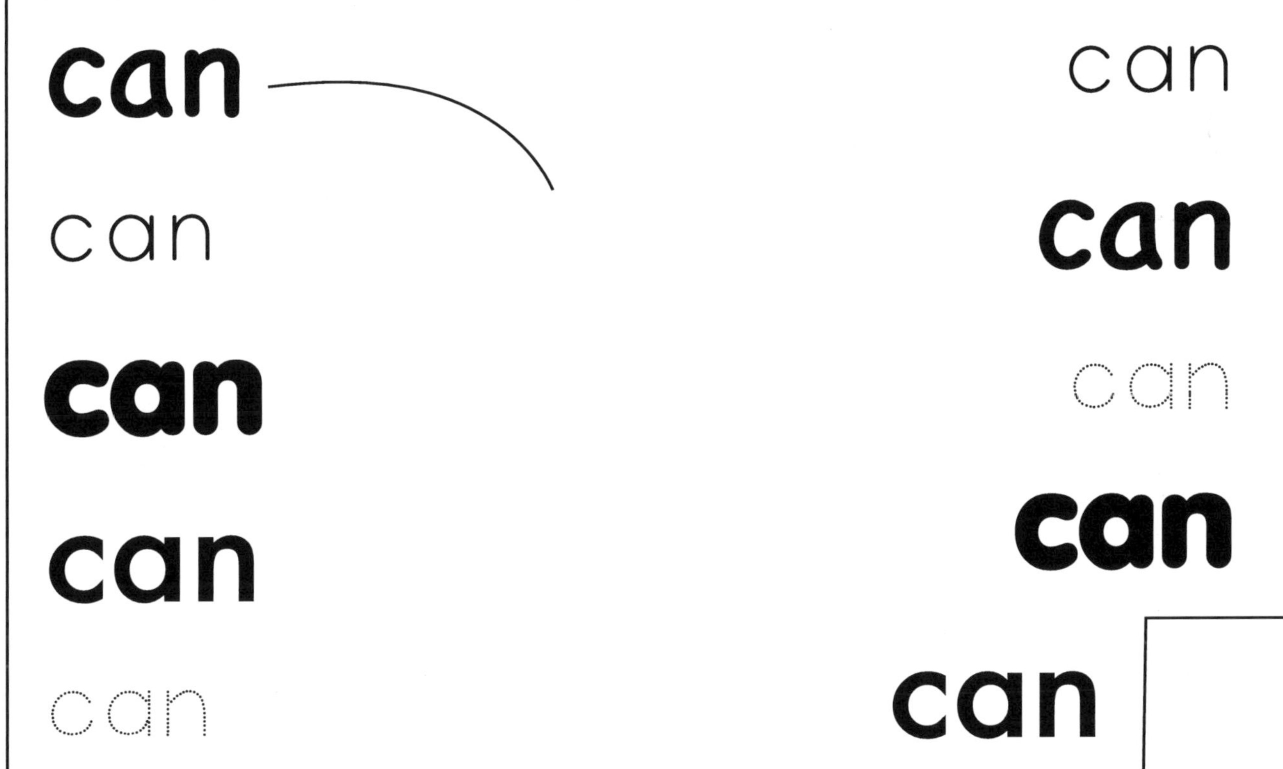

Amazing! Let's review and play a game.

FIND THE MATCHING WORD

Read the sentence in the picture and then read the list of words on the right side. Find the word that best fits the sentence and then pencil in the missing word in the space provided.

BUG SWAT GAME

This game is best played with 2 or more players. One adult/reader reads the word out loud and the 2+ players race to find the word on the page. The first person to swat the the bug with their hands wins the round. Continue until you have gone through all of the sight words you are practicing.

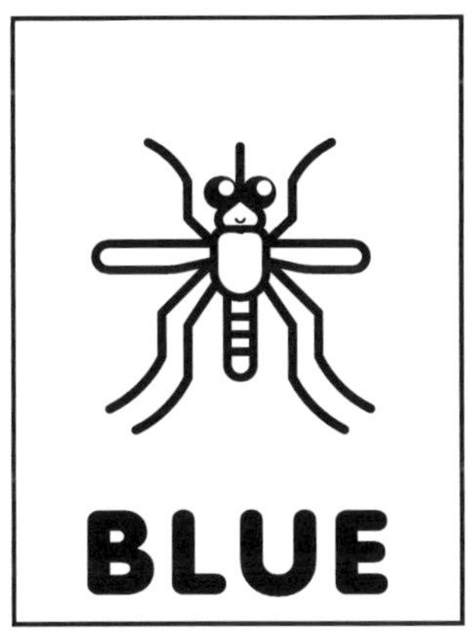

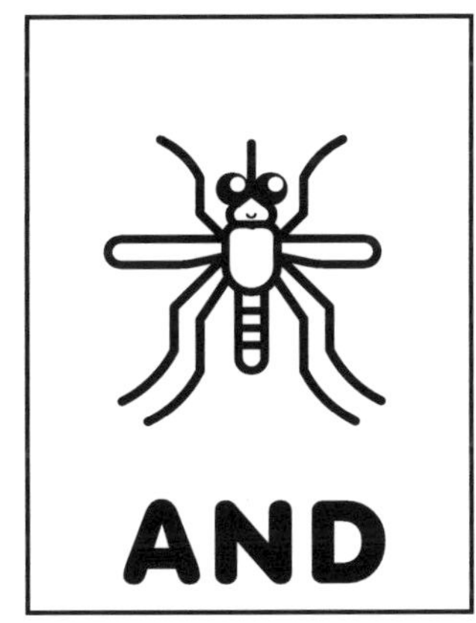

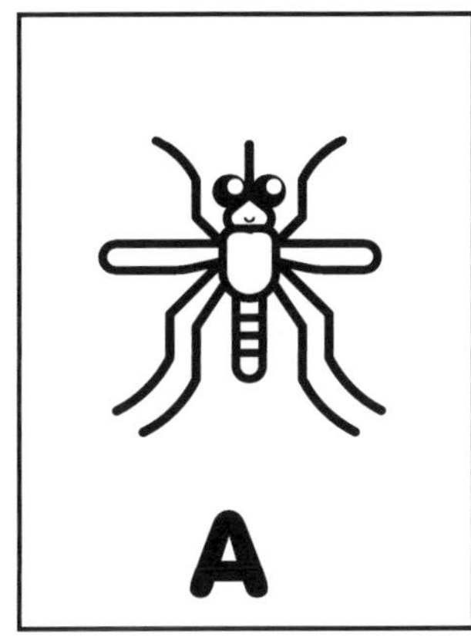

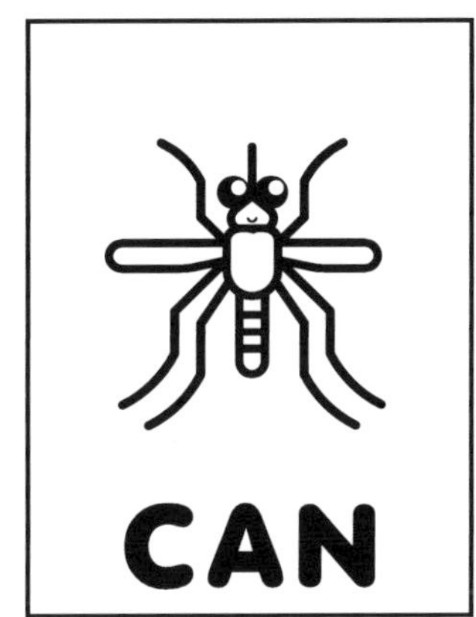

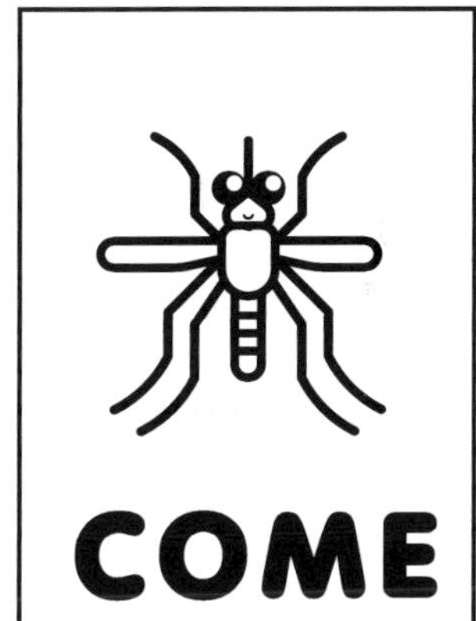

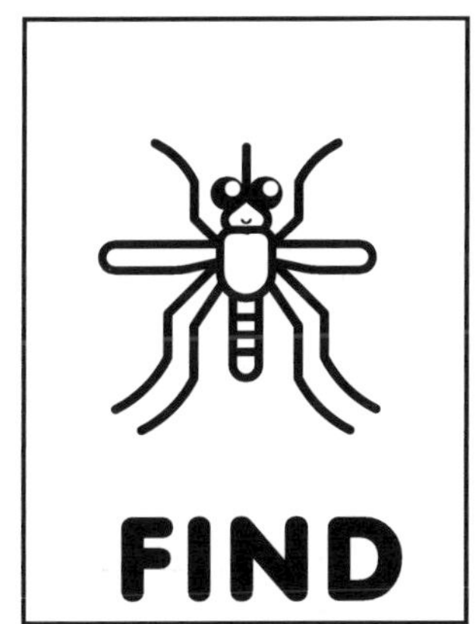

SAY & SPELL

Today we are going to learn the word 'come'. I'll read the word out loud and show you the direction the arrow goes with my finger. Then it will be your turn. Let's do this 3 times.

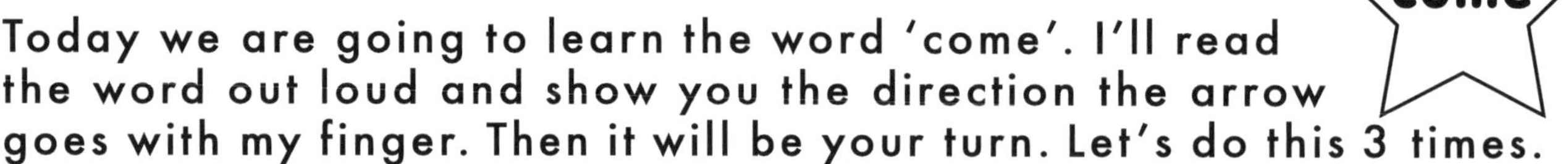

That's great! come. I will come to the party.

Now let's learn to SPELL our new word. Say the new word out loud again but this time, spell out the letters. Let's do this 3 times.

Fantastic!

Now that you can say and spell the word, let's practice tracing the letters. Using your pointer finger, trace each letter in the sky in front of you. Let's do this 3 times.

PRINT & RECOGNIZE

Now it's time to practice printing on paper. With your pencil, trace the dots and then practice on your own.

come come

Let's see if we can recognize the words in the picture below. Color all of the rays of the rainbow that have the word 'come' in them. Hint: There should be 3 rays to color.

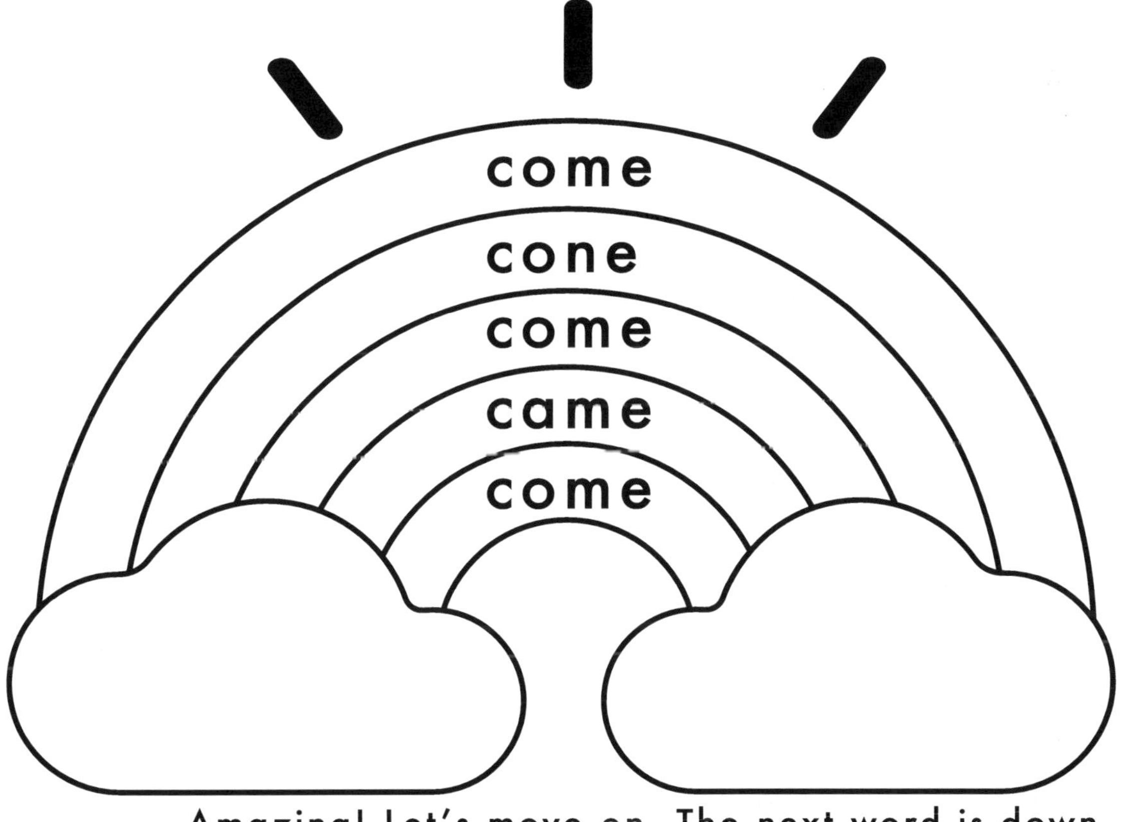

Amazing! Let's move on. The next word is down.

SAY & SPELL

down

Today we are going to learn the word 'down'. I'll read the word out loud and show you the direction the arrow goes with my finger. Then it will be your turn. Let's do this 3 times.

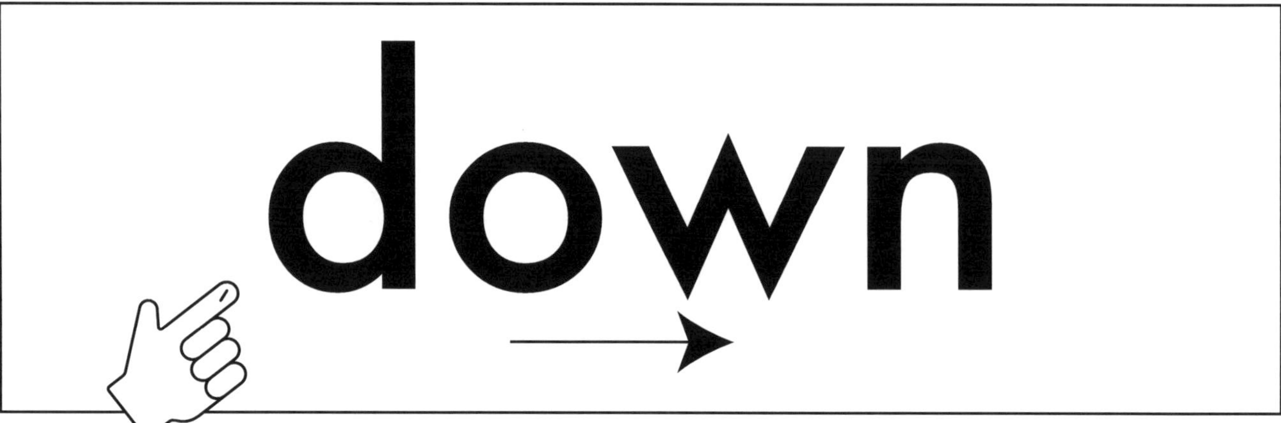

That's great! down. I jumped down the stairs.

Now let's learn to SPELL our new word. Say the new word out loud again but this time, spell out the letters. Let's do this 3 times.

d o w n

Fantastic!

Now that you can say and spell the word, let's practice tracing the letters. Using your pointer finger, trace each letter in the sky in front of you. Let's do this 3 times.

PRINT & RECOGNIZE

Now it's time to practice printing on paper. With your pencil, trace the dots and then practice on your own.

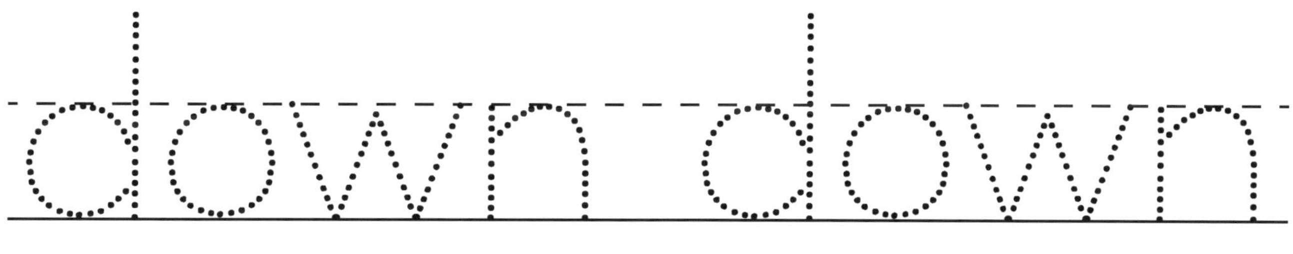

Let's see if we can make our way out of the maze by following the word 'down'. When you come across the word, read it out loud. Beware of similar words, as they will not lead you to the exit.

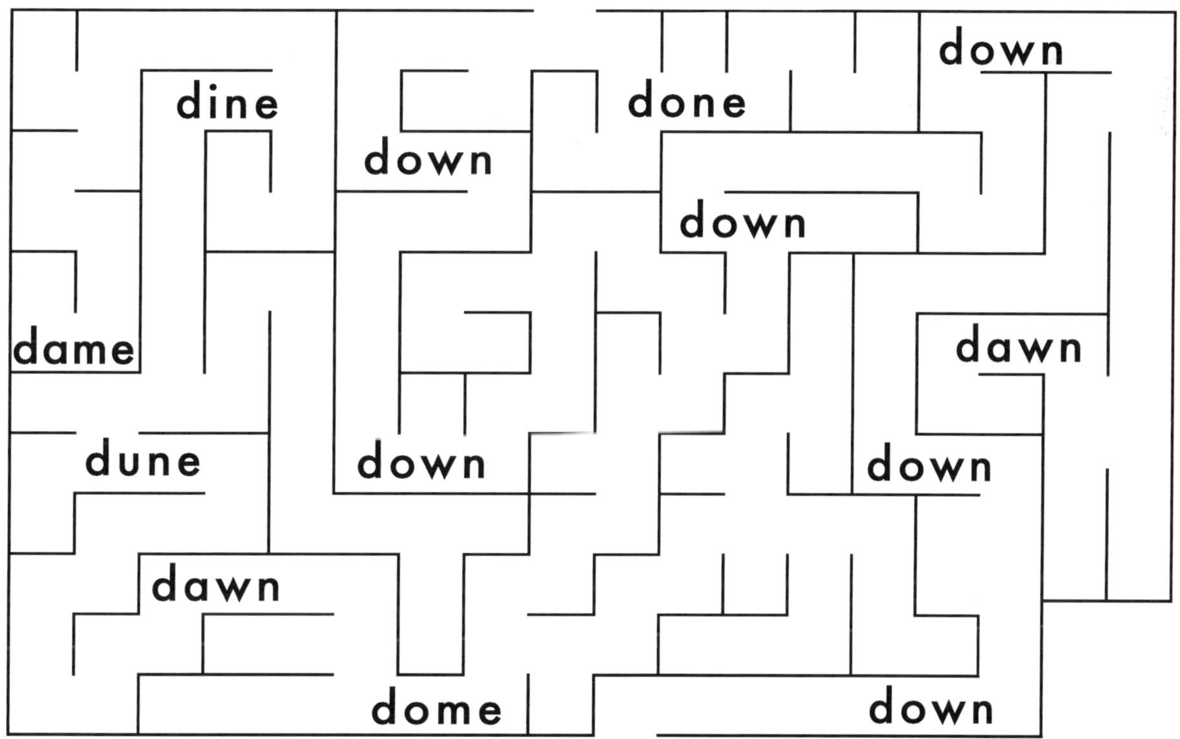

Amazing! Let's move on. The next word is find.

SAY & SPELL

find

The next word we are going to learn is 'find'. I'll read the word out loud and show you the direction the arrow goes with my finger. Then it will be your turn. Let's do this 3 times.

That's great! find. I am trying to find my shoes.

Now let's learn to SPELL our new word. Say the new word out loud again but this time, spell out the letters. Let's do this 3 times.

Fantastic!

Now that you can say and spell the word, let's practice tracing the letters. Using your pointer finger, trace each letter in the sky in front of you. Let's do this 3 times.

PRINT & RECOGNIZE

Now it's time to practice printing on paper. With your pencil, trace the dots and then practice on your own.

find find

Let's now practice filling in the missing letters to our new word below. Each word is the word 'find'. Decide which letters are missing and fill them into the spaces provided.

f _ _ d	_ i n d
f _ n d	f i _ _
_ _ n d	f i n _

Amazing! Let's review and play a game.

FIND THE MATCHING WORD

Read the sentences below and find the matching word from the list. Write in the missing word and say it out loud.

come	blue	down	find	big	can

1. Can you please ______ here?

2. Come ______ from the tree.

3. I will help you ______ the cat.

4. He is in the ______ tree.

5. He has a ______ collar on.

6. I ______ get him for you.

SIGHT WORD BOARD GAME

Roll the dice to see which word you land on. When you land on that word, say the word out loud, and try to use it in a sentence. Keep going until the first person makes it to the end as the winner!

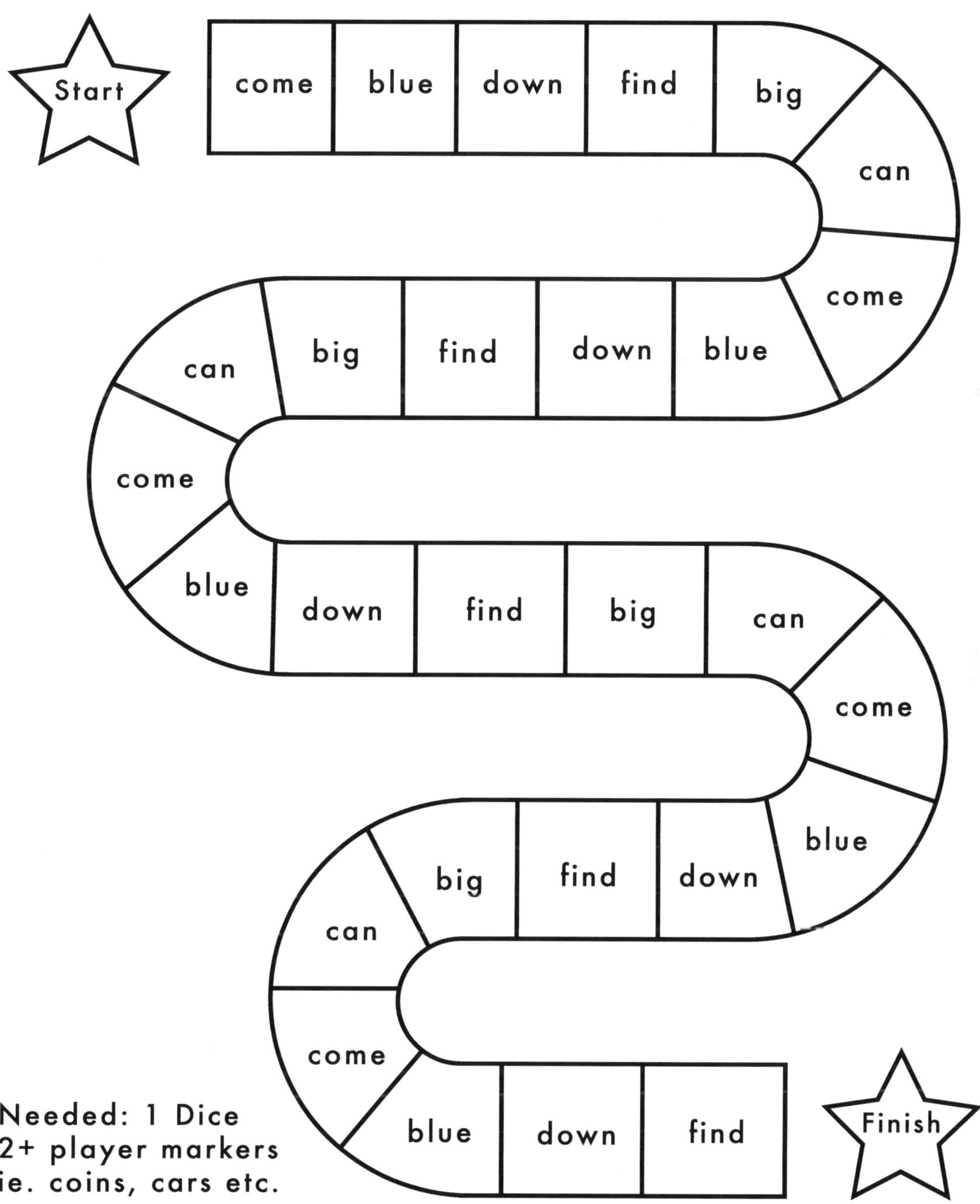

Needed: 1 Dice
2+ player markers
ie. coins, cars etc.

SAY & SPELL

Today we are going to learn the word 'for'. I'll read the word out loud and show you the direction the arrow goes with my finger. Then it will be your turn. Let's do this 3 times.

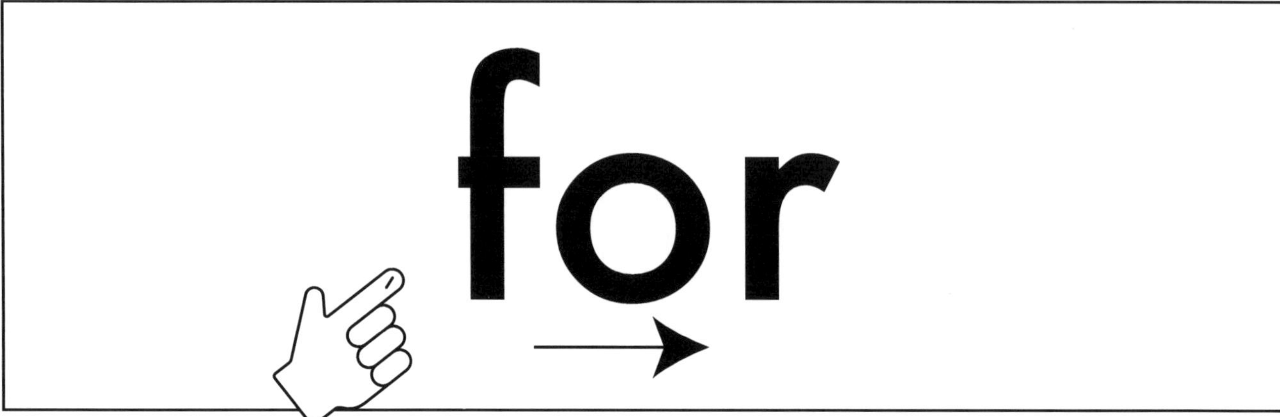

That's great! for. This present is for my friend.

Now let's learn to SPELL our new word. Say the new word out loud again but this time, spell out the letters. Let's do this 3 times.

Fantastic!

Now that you can say and spell the word, let's practice tracing the letters. Using your pointer finger, trace each letter in the sky in front of you. Let's do this 3 times.

PRINT & RECOGNIZE

Now it's time to practice printing on paper. With your pencil, trace the dots and then practice on your own.

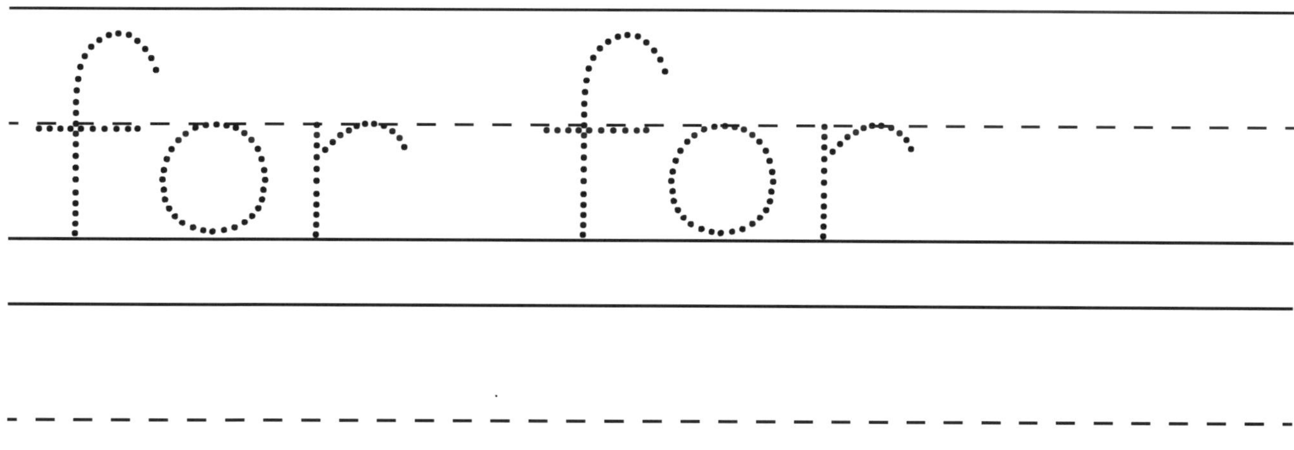

To really remember our new word, let's see if we can recognize the word among other words that look similar. Find the 4 words that do not belong and write them in the spaces provided below.

for	far	for	for	for
fair	for	for	fur	for
for	fort	for	for	for

Amazing! Let's move on. The next word is funny.

SAY & SPELL

funny

Today we are going to learn the word 'funny'. I'll read the word out loud and show you the direction the arrow goes with my finger. Then it will be your turn. Let's do this 3 times.

That's great! funny. You are too funny!

Now let's learn to SPELL our new word. Say the new word out loud again but this time, spell out the letters. Let's do this 3 times.

f u n n y

Fantastic!

Now that you can say and spell the word, let's practice tracing the letters. Using your pointer finger, trace each letter in the sky in front of you. Let's do this 3 times.

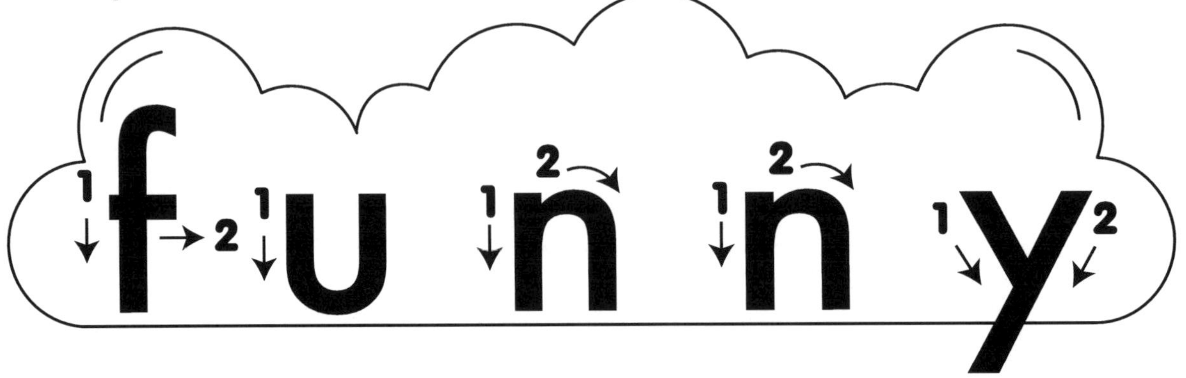

PRINT & RECOGNIZE

Now it's time to practice printing on paper. With your pencil, trace the dots and then practice on your own.

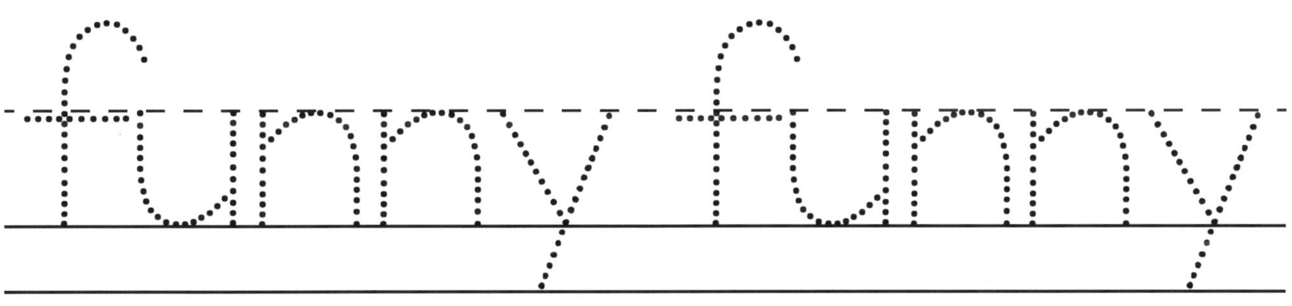

All of the sea animals have come to meet you. Can you help color in the ones with the word 'funny' on them? Hint: There are 3 sea animals to color.

Amazing! Let's move on. The next word is go.

SAY & SPELL

go

The next word we are going to learn is 'go'. I'll read the word out loud and show you the direction the arrow goes with my finger. Then it will be your turn. Let's do this 3 times.

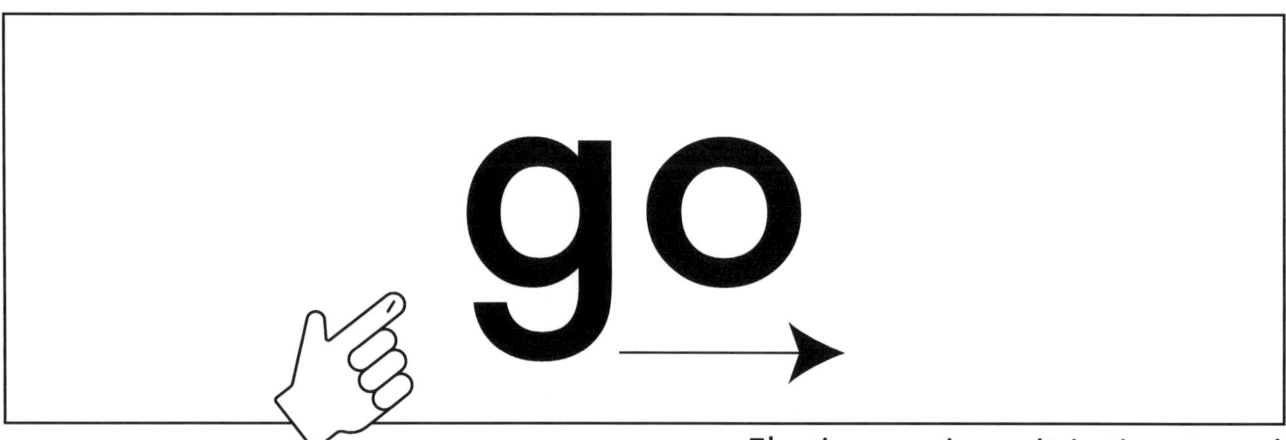

That's great! go. It is time to go!

Now let's learn to SPELL our new word. Say the new word out loud again but this time, spell out the letters. Let's do this 3 times.

Fantastic!

Now that you can say and spell the word, let's practice tracing the letters. Using your pointer finger, trace each letter in the sky in front of you. Let's do this 3 times.

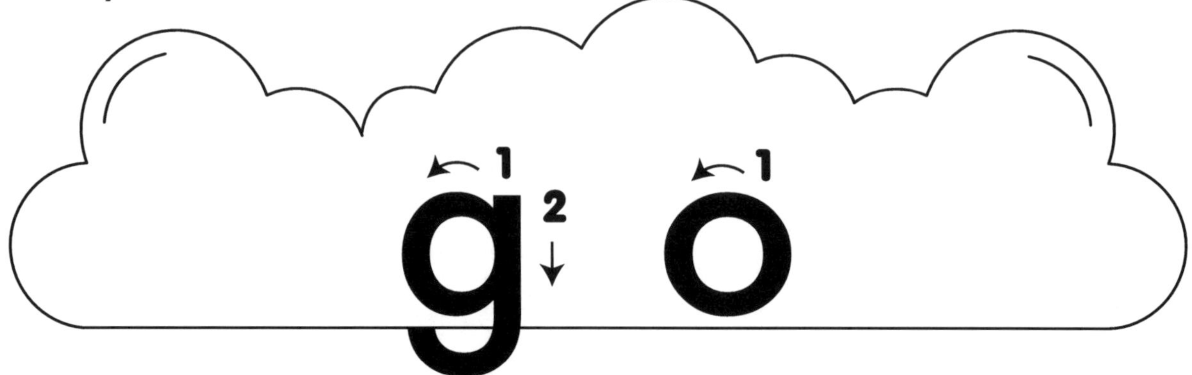

PRINT & RECOGNIZE

Now it's time to practice printing on paper. With your pencil, trace the dots and then practice on your own.

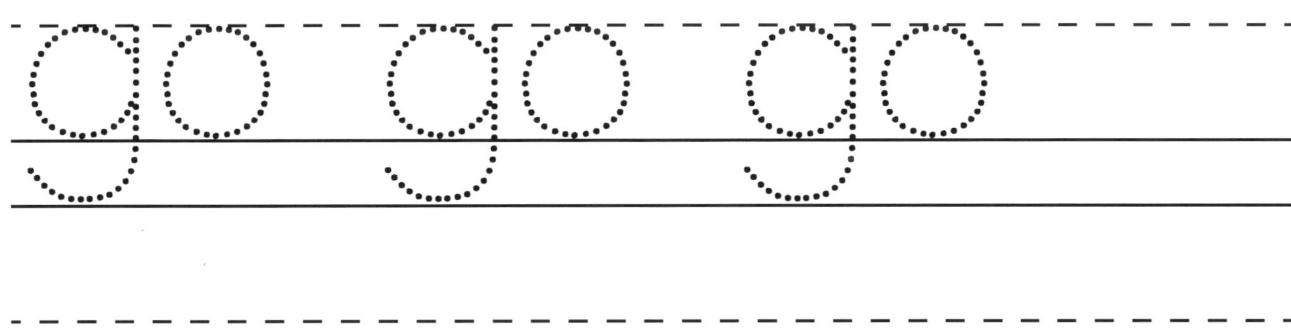

Let's see if we can recognize the words in the picture below. Circle all of the circles that have the word go in them. Then color them all in. Hint: There are 3 circles to color.

Amazing! Let's review and play a game.

READ AND DRAW

Read the words in the boxes and find the matching shape in the legend to the right. Draw the matching shapes around the words until you have completed the full chart. To make it more challenging, use the word in a different sentence each time.

for	go	funny	for	◇ for
funny	go	for	for	
for	funny	go	go	○ go
for	funny	funny	for	
for	go	go	funny	☆ funny
funny	go	for	go	

THE DOT GAME

This game is played by drawing a line connecting 2 dots. Players take turns drawing a line until they have completed drawing a box. After a box is made. they can write a word in the box. The first person to draw 3 boxes and write the 3 words below wins.

for	funny	go

SAY & SPELL

help

Today we are going to learn the word 'help'. I'll read the word out loud and show you the direction the arrow goes with my finger. Then it will be your turn. Let's do this 3 times.

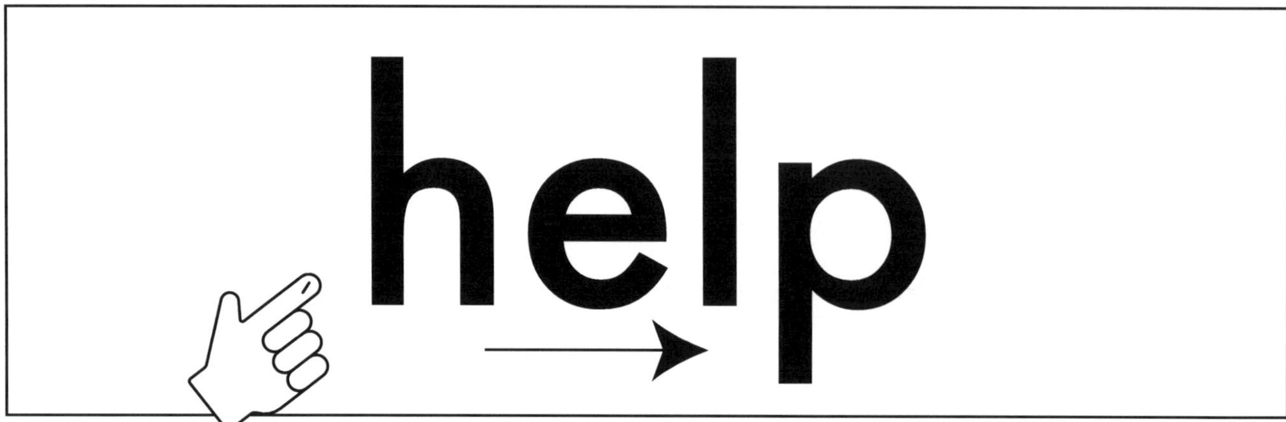

That's great! help. I would love to help.

Now let's learn to SPELL our new word. Say the new word out loud again but this time, spell out the letters. Let's do this 3 times.

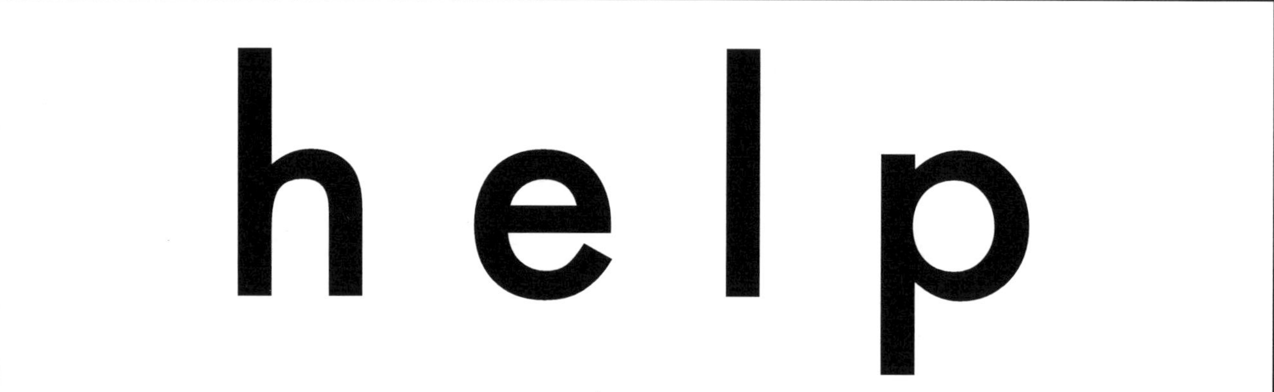

Fantastic!

Now that you can say and spell the word, let's practice tracing the letters. Using your pointer finger, trace each letter in the sky in front of you. Let's do this 3 times.

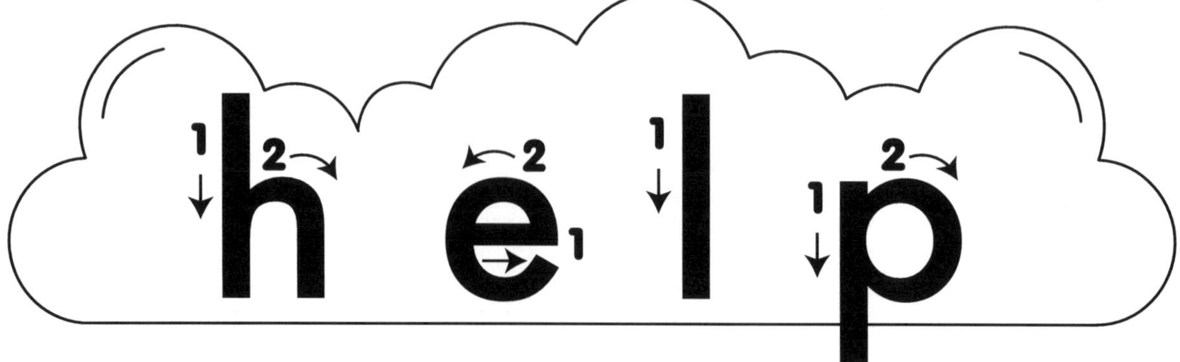

PRINT & RECOGNIZE

Now it's time to practice printing on paper. With your pencil, trace the dots and then practice on your own.

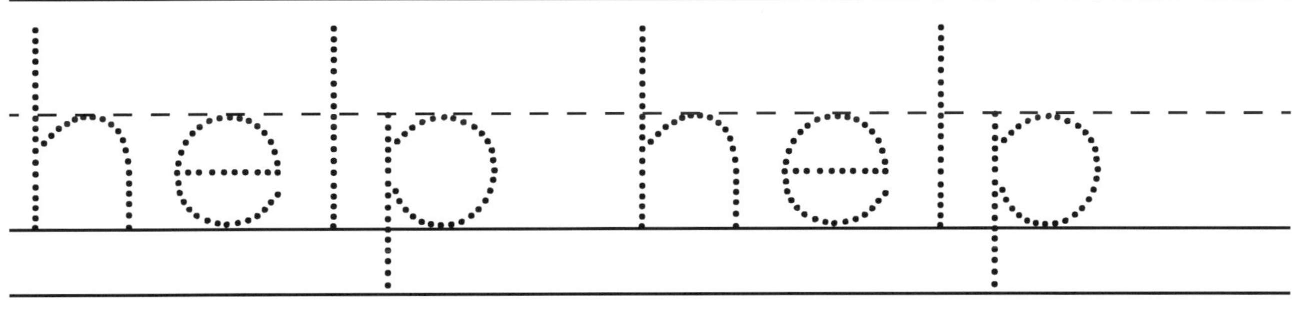

Let's see if we can recognize the words in the picture below. Find the word 'help' in the word search below and circle the letters. Hint: The word is in the search 4 times.

h	a	b	u	f	h	r
e	h	e	l	p	e	o
l	g	o	s	a	l	u
p	k	h	e	l	p	

Amazing! Let's move on. The next word is here.

SAY & SPELL

Today we are going to learn the word here. I'll read the word out loud and show you the direction the arrow goes with my finger. Then it will be your turn. Let's do this 3 times.

here

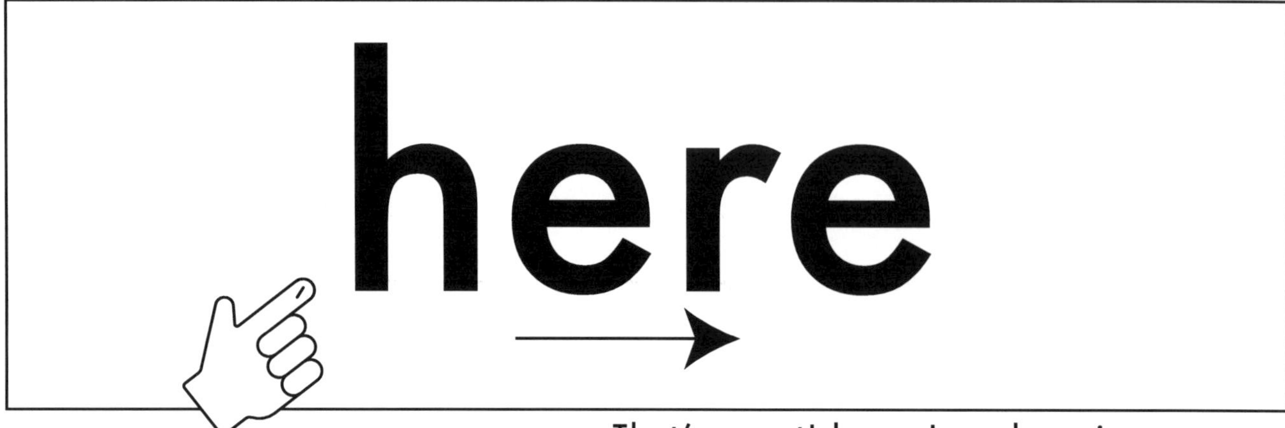

That's great! here. I am here in my room.

Now let's learn to SPELL our new word. Say the new word out loud again but this time, spell out the letters. Let's do this 3 times.

Fantastic!

Now that you can say and spell the word, let's practice tracing the letters. Using your pointer finger, trace each letter in the sky in front of you. Let's do this 3 times.

PRINT & RECOGNIZE

Now it's time to practice printing on paper. With your pencil, trace the dots and then practice on your own.

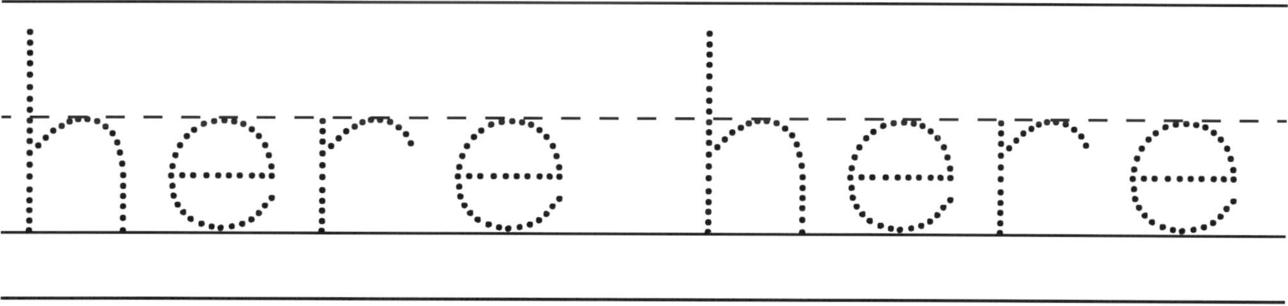

Let's see if we can recognize the words in the picture below. Match all of the different ways the word 'here' can be written by drawing a line between pairs that match.

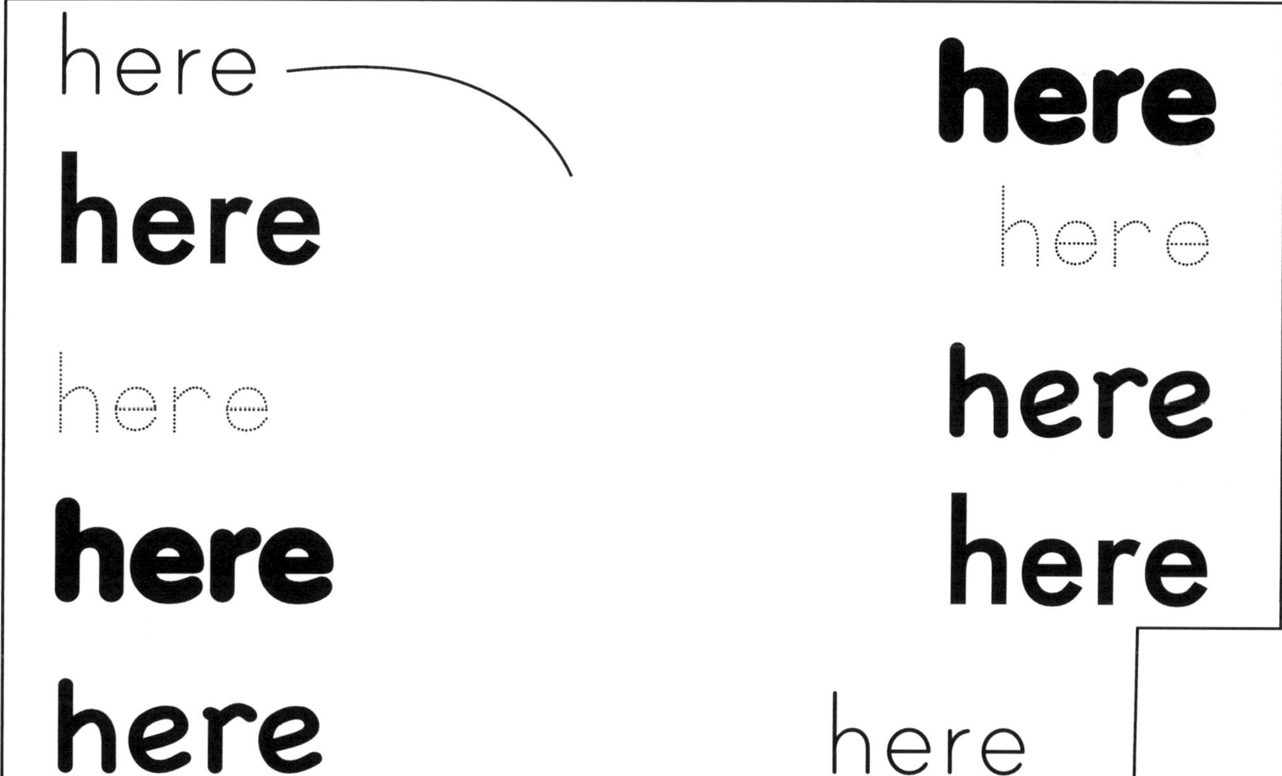

Amazing! Let's move on. The next word is I.

SAY & SPELL

I

The next word we are going to learn is I. I'll read the word out loud and show you the direction the arrow goes with my finger. Then it will be your turn. Let's do this 3 times.

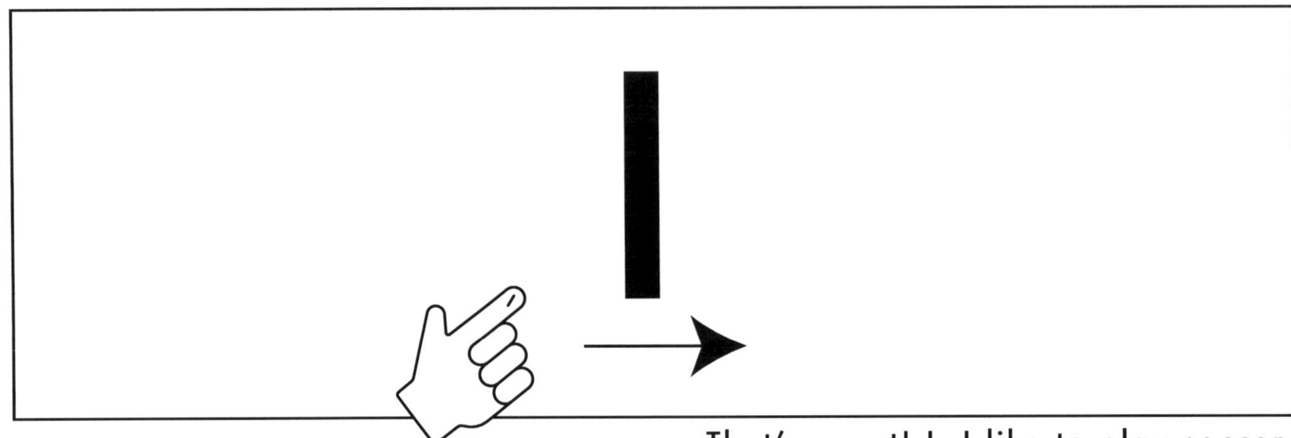

That's great! I. I like to play soccer.

Now let's learn to SPELL our new word. Say the new word out loud again but this time, spell out the letters. Let's do this 3 times.

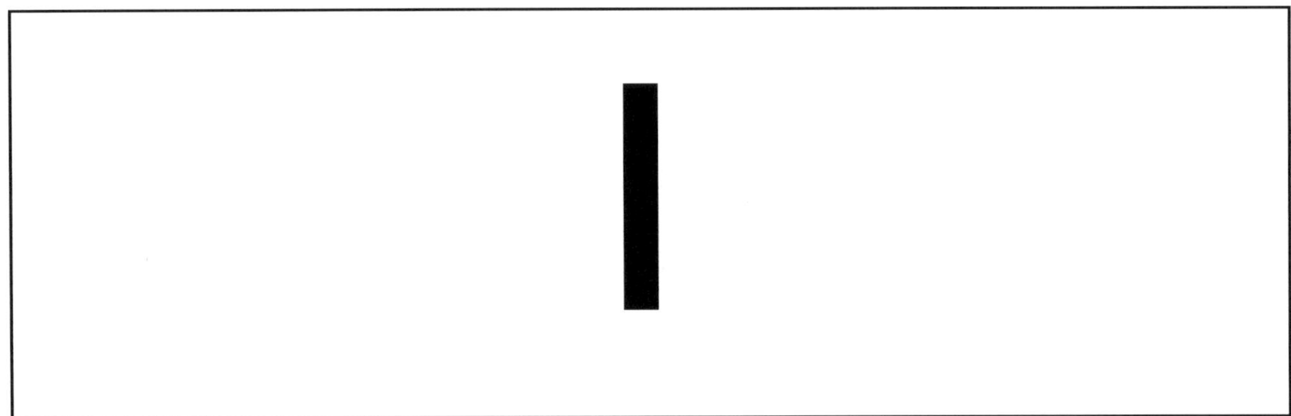

Fantastic!

Now that you can say and spell the word, let's practice tracing the letters. Using your pointer finger, trace each letter in the sky in front of you. Let's do this 3 times.

PRINT & RECOGNIZE

Now it's time to practice printing on paper. With your pencil, trace the dots and then practice on your own.

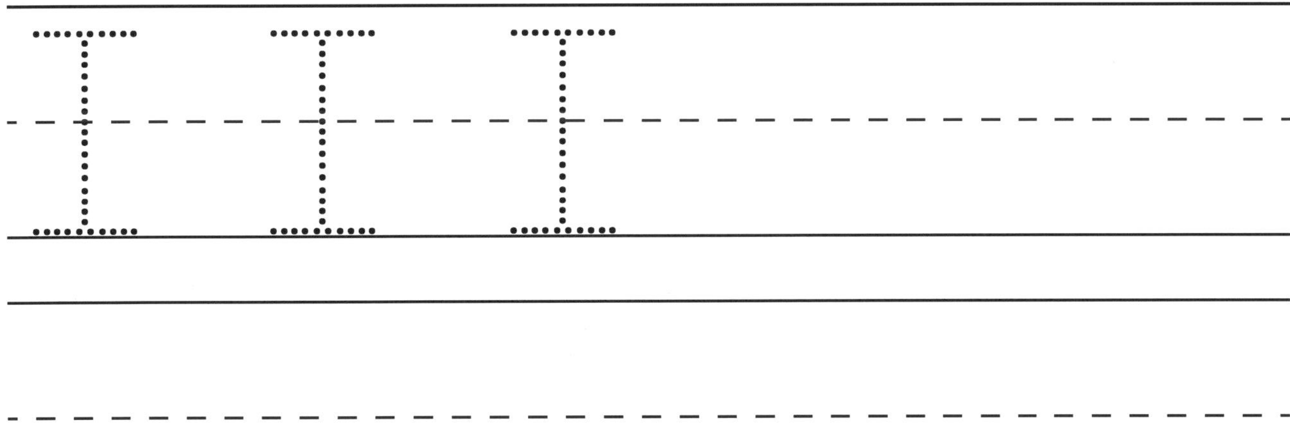

Let's figure out the image below by connecting all of the dots with the word 'I'. Stay away from similar words as they will not help you complete the image. Hint: The image is seen in the sky.

T L I I I L T J T I I I I I I I I I I I I I I T

Amazing! Let's review and play a game.

MONSTER PIXEL ART

Match the words in the squares to the colors in the legend to create a pixel monster. Fully color in the squares to reveal the hidden monster. Read the words out loud and try to use them in a sentence about the monster.

COLOR CHART	here: lime green	I: black	help: blue

here	here	help	here	here	here	here	help	here	here
here	here	here	help	here	here	help	here	here	here
here	help	help					help	help	here
here	help	help		I	I		help	help	here
here	help	help					help	help	here
here	help		help	help	help	help		help	here
here	help	help					help	help	here
here	help	help	help	help	help	help	help	help	here
here	here	here	here	help	help	here	here	here	here
here	here	here	here	help	help	here	here	here	here

SPIDER WEB GAME

Using the same rules as hangman, one person chooses a word and writes it on a hidden piece of paper. They then write a line for each letter the word has. The next person has to guess the letters of the word. If you get a letter right, write it in where the letter would go. If you guess an incorrect letter, draw one part of the spider onto the web until you have either guessed the word correctly or drawn all parts of the spider. It is then the next person's turn.

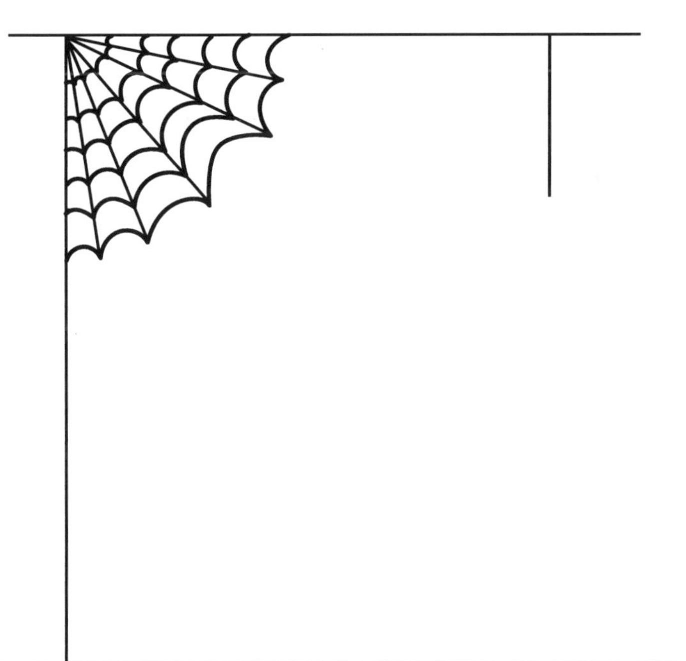

a b c d e f g h i j

k l m n o p q r s

t u v w x y z

___ ___ ___ ___

SAY & SPELL

in

Today we are going to learn the word 'in'. I'll read the word out loud and show you the direction the arrow goes with my finger. Then it will be your turn. Let's do this 3 times.

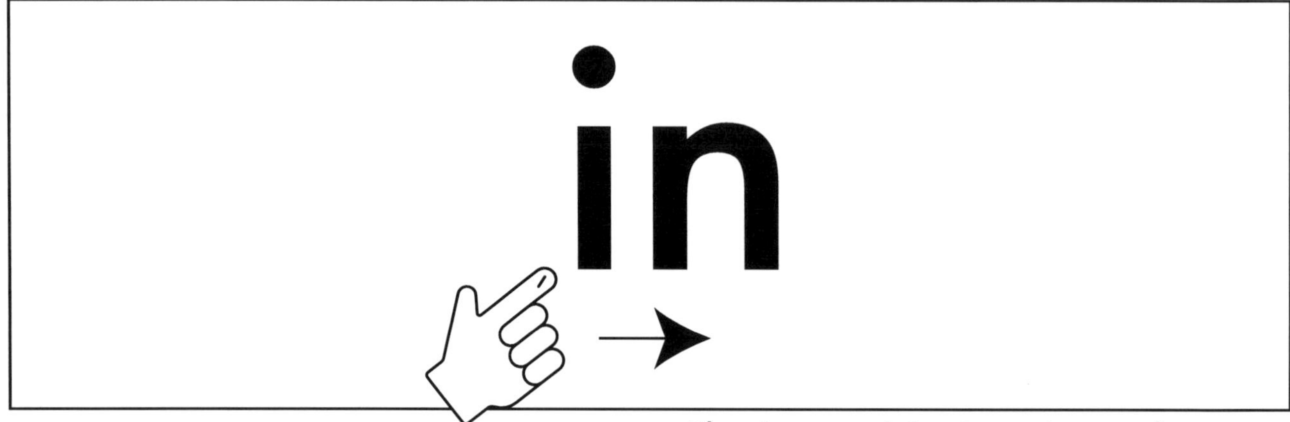

That's great! in. I am in a relay race.

Now let's learn to SPELL our new word. Say the new word out loud again but this time, spell out the letters. Let's do this 3 times.

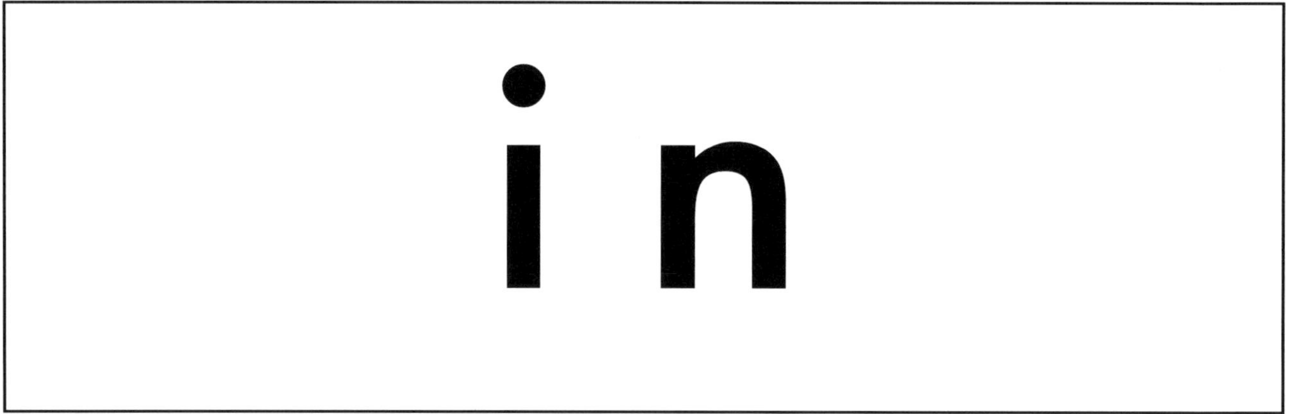

Fantastic!

Now that you can say and spell the word, let's practice tracing the letters. Using your pointer finger, trace each letter in the sky in front of you. Let's do this 3 times.

PRINT & RECOGNIZE

Now it's time to practice printing on paper. With your pencil, trace the dots and then practice on your own.

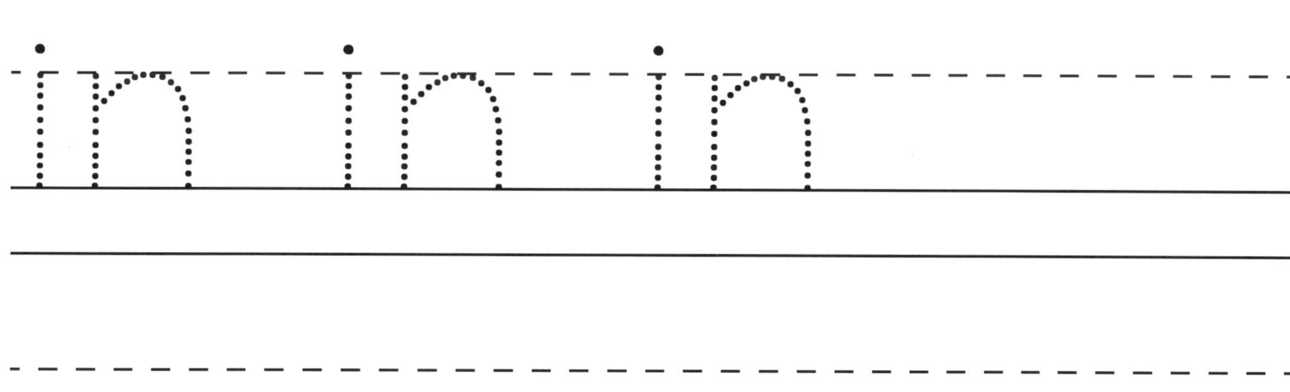

Let's see if we can spot the difference between our new word 'in' and similar words below. Color in the outer space picture by matching the colors in the index below, to the words in the picture.

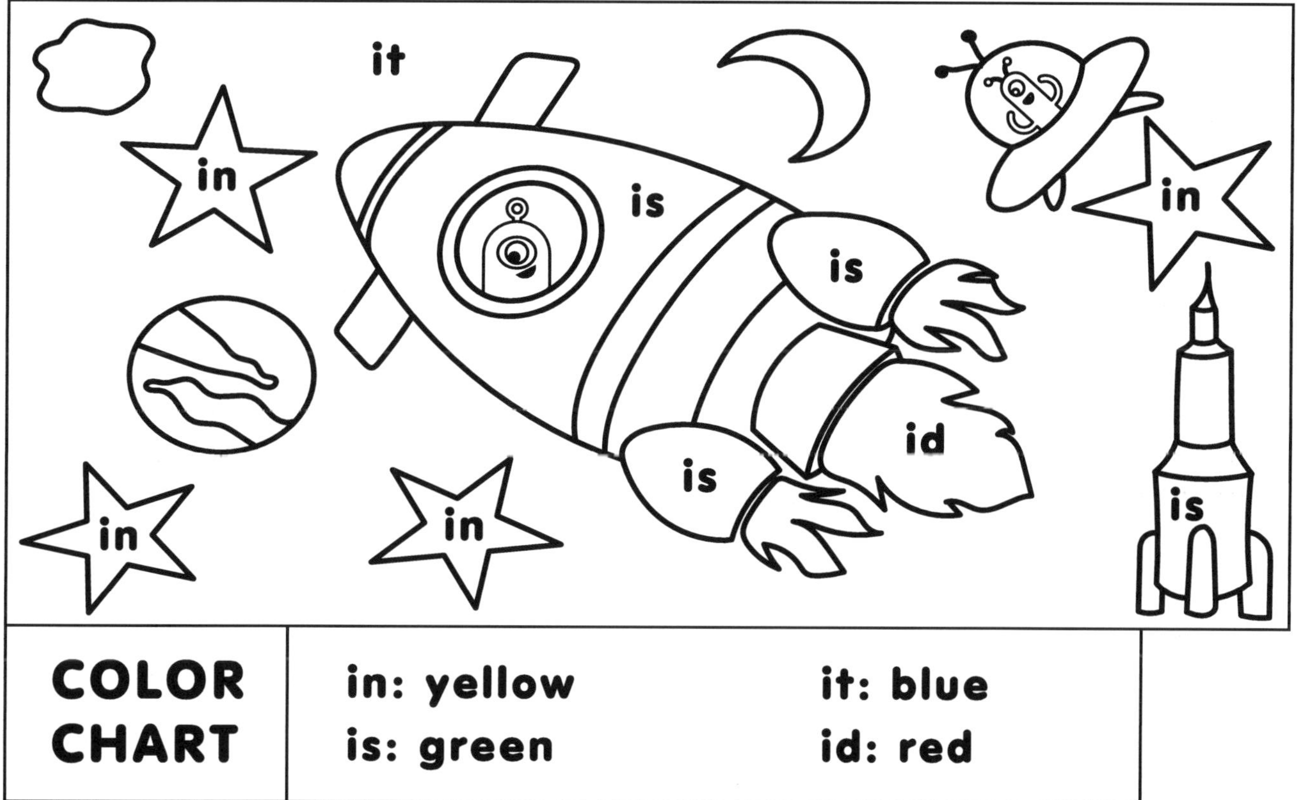

COLOR CHART	in: yellow	it: blue
	is: green	id: red

Amazing! Let's move on. The next word is is.

SAY & SPELL

Today we are going to learn the word 'is'. I'll read the word out loud and show you the direction the arrow goes with my finger. Then it will be your turn. Let's do this 3 times.

is

That's great! is. This is a delicious cake.

Now let's learn to SPELL our new word. Say the new word out loud again but this time, spell out the letters. Let's do this 3 times.

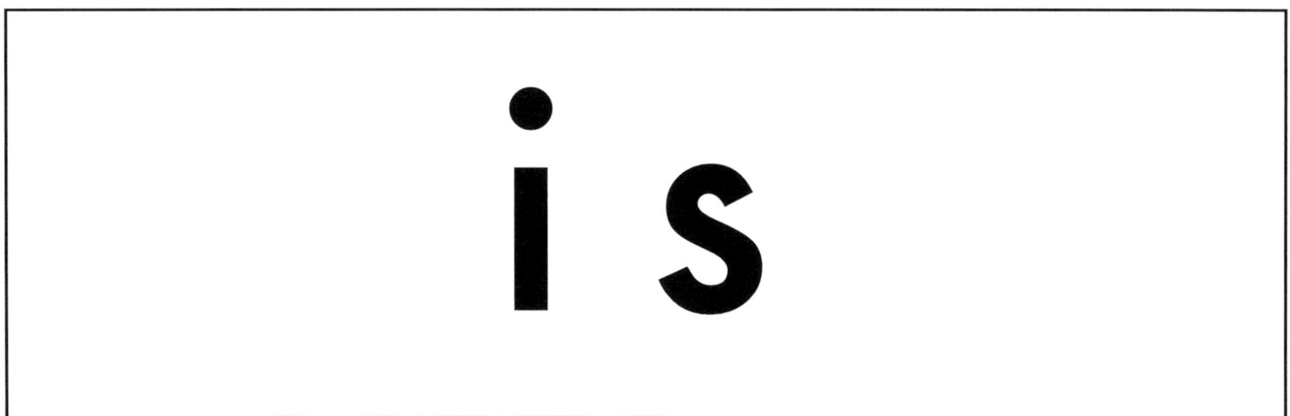

Fantastic!

Now that you can say and spell the word, let's practice tracing the letters. Using your pointer finger, trace each letter in the sky in front of you. Let's do this 3 times.

PRINT & RECOGNIZE

Now it's time to practice printing on paper. With your pencil, trace the dots and then practice on your own.

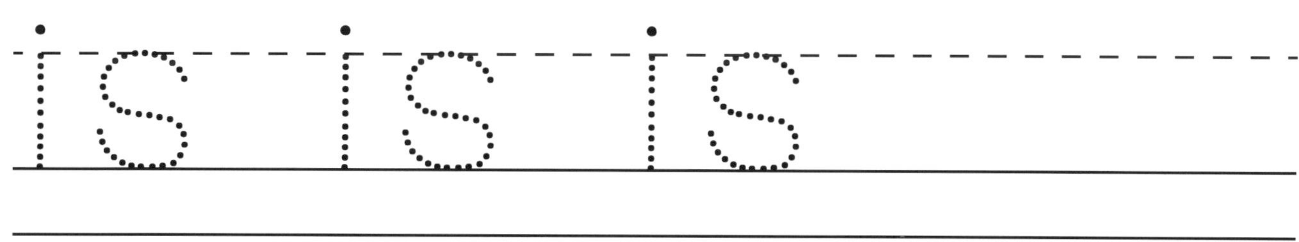

Let's see if we can help the bees get out of the honeycomb by following the word 'is'. When you come across the word, read it out loud. Beware of similar words, as they will not lead you to the exit.

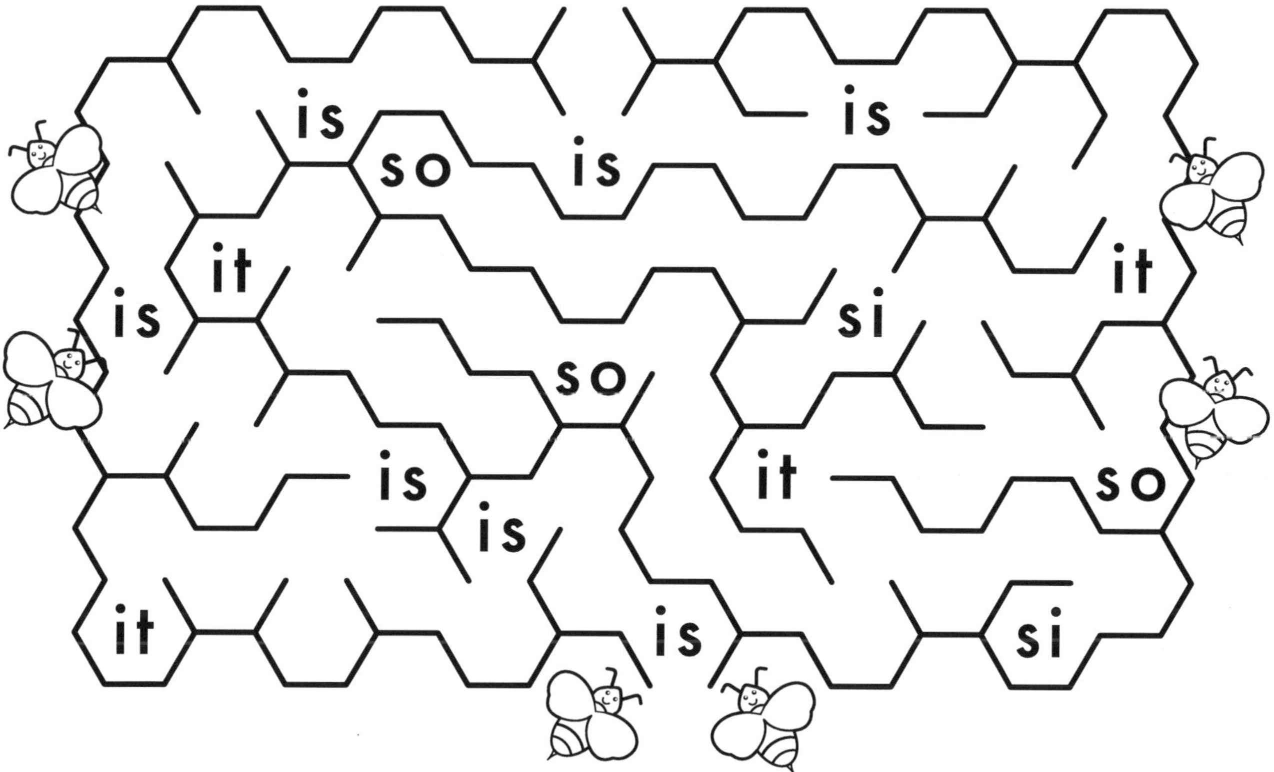

Amazing! Let's move on. The next word is it.

SAY & SPELL

The next word we are going to learn is 'it'. I'll read the word out loud and show you the direction the arrow goes with my finger. Then it will be your turn. Let's do this 3 times.

That's great! it. I will go and find it.

Now let's learn to SPELL our new word. Say the new word out loud again but this time, spell out the letters. Let's do this 3 times.

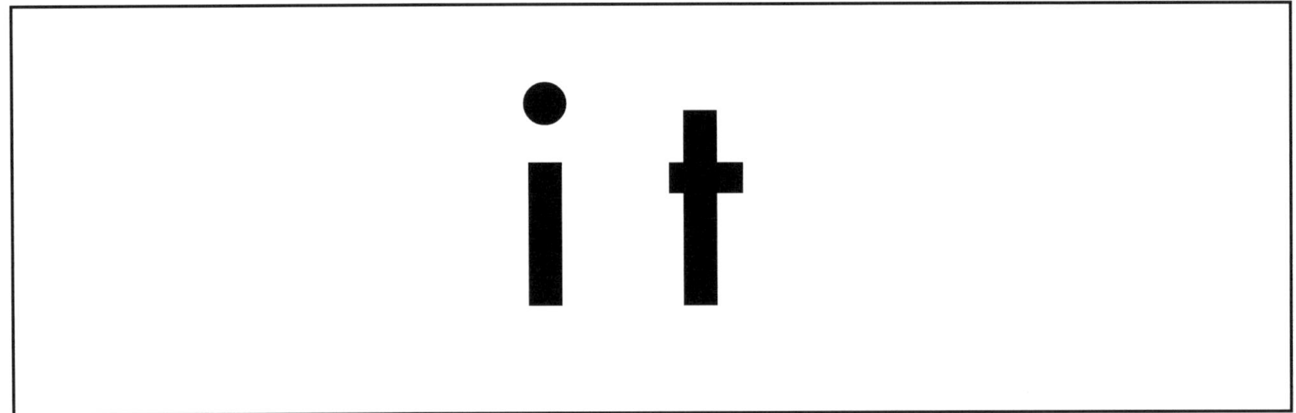

Fantastic!

Now that you can say and spell the word, let's practice tracing the letters. Using your pointer finger, trace each letter in the sky in front of you. Let's do this 3 times.

PRINT & RECOGNIZE

Now it's time to practice printing on paper. With your pencil, trace the dots and then practice on your own.

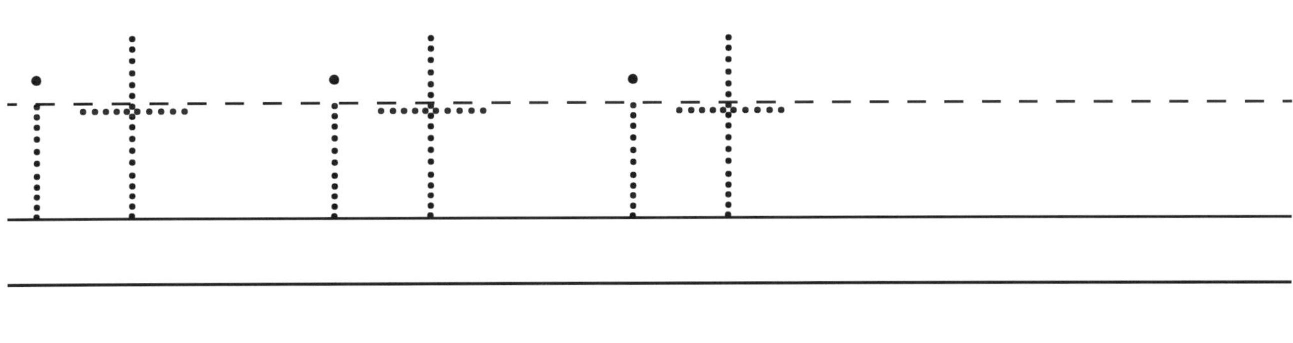

Let's see if we can find the word 'it' among similar looking words. Read the words below and circle the word 'it' when you come across it. Hint: the word should be found 3 times.

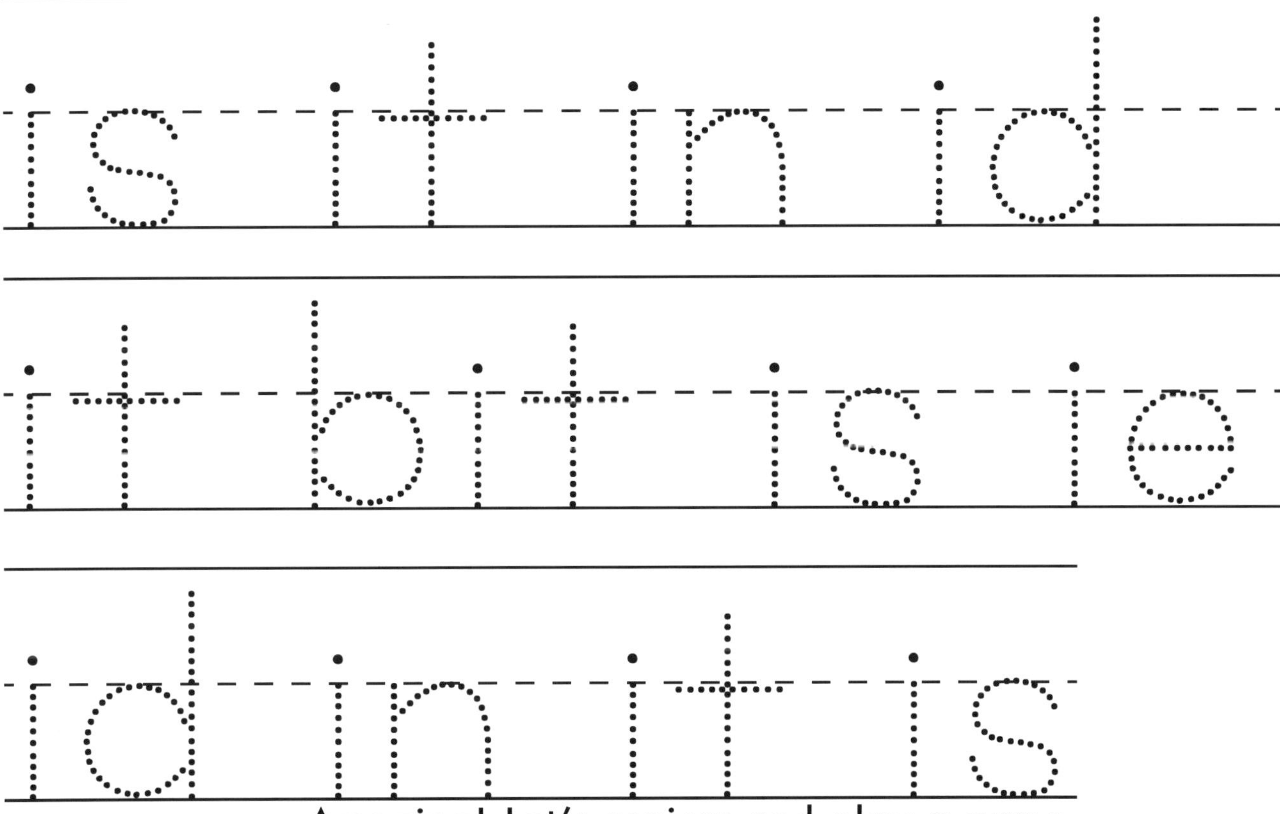

Amazing! Let's review and play a game.

BUBBLE GUM MACHINE

Match the words on the bubble gum balls to the words in the legend. Read the word out loud and use it in a sentence. Color the bubble gum balls in the colors from the legend to fill up your candy machine.

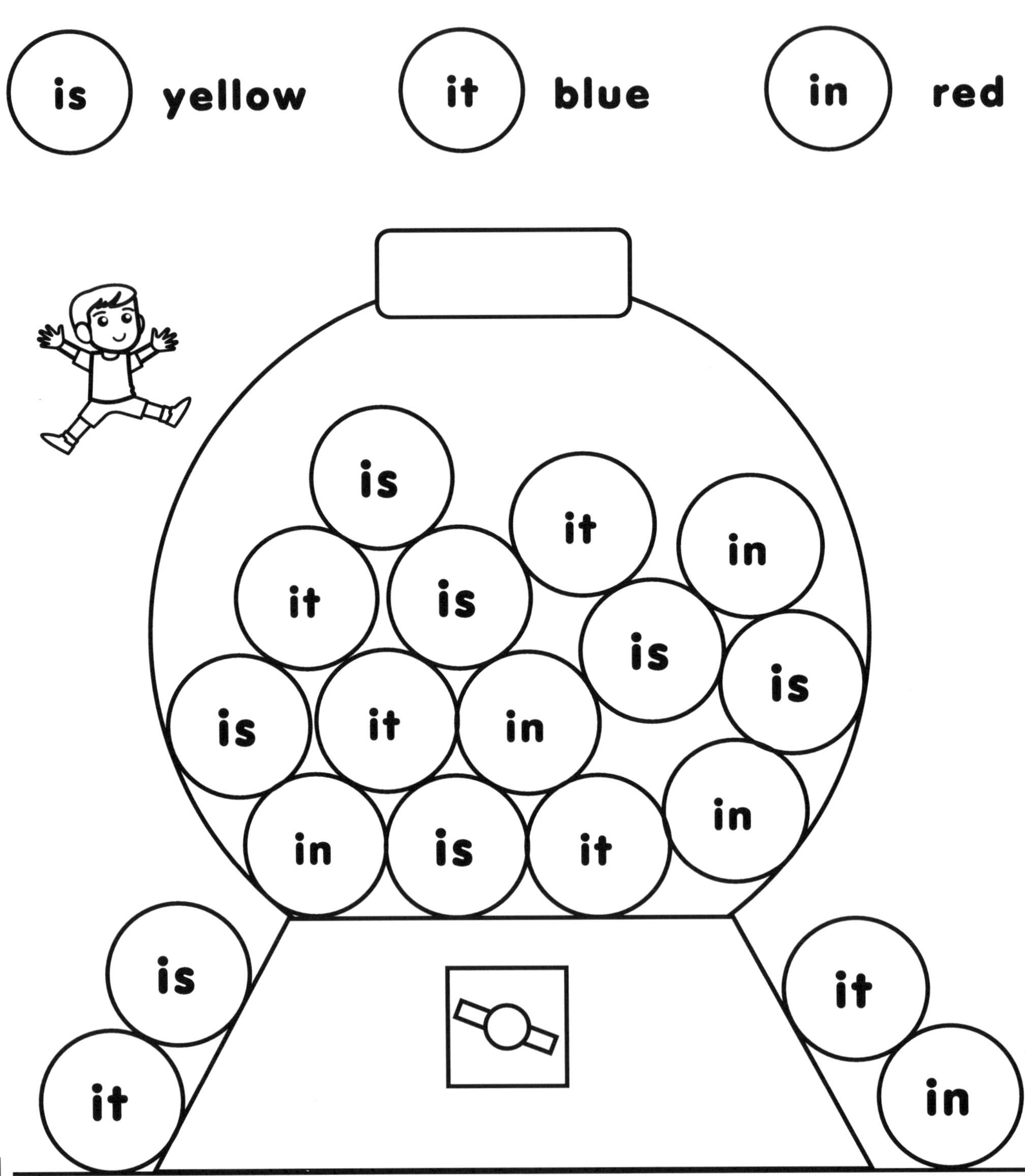

SNAKES & LADDERS GAME

This game is played the same way as regular snakes and ladders. Take turns to roll your dice. Move a coin along the board. When you land on a word, read it out loud. If you can't read the word, skip a turn. Play until someone wins the game.

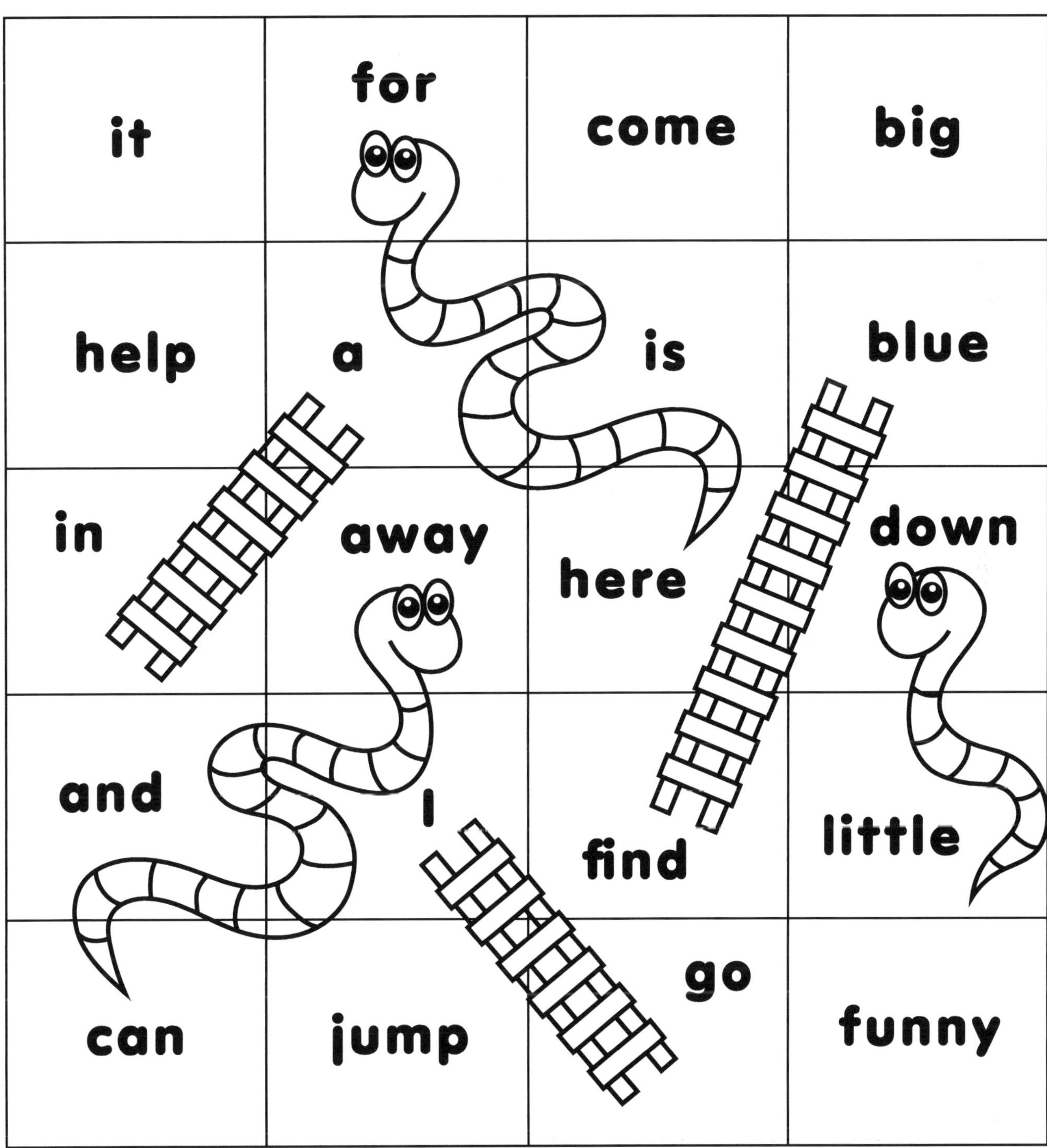

SAY & SPELL

jump

Today we are going to learn the word 'jump'. I'll read the word out loud and show you the direction the arrow goes with my finger. Then it will be your turn. Let's do this 3 times.

That's great! jump. I can jump really high!

Now let's learn to SPELL our new word. Say the new word out loud again but this time, spell out the letters. Let's do this 3 times.

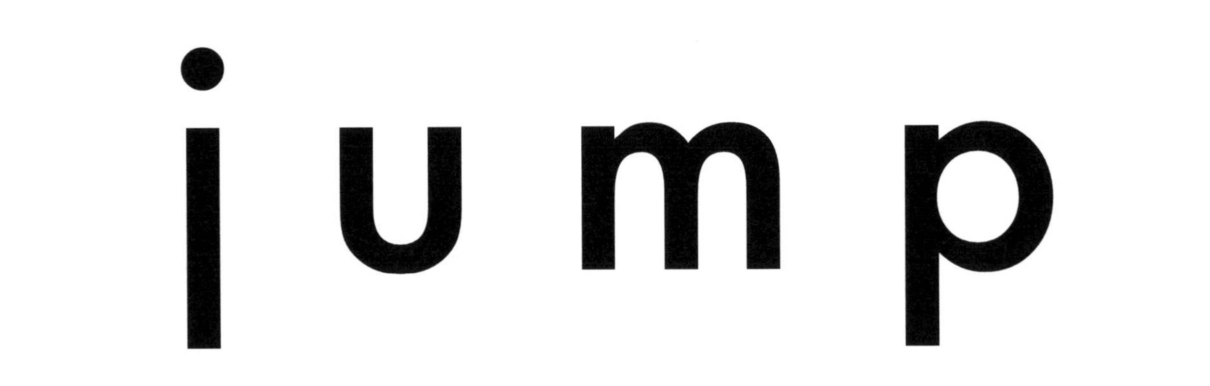

Fantastic!

Now that you can say and spell the word, let's practice tracing the letters. Using your pointer finger, trace each letter in the sky in front of you. Let's do this 3 times.

PRINT & RECOGNIZE

Now it's time to practice printing on paper. With your pencil, trace the dots and then practice on your own.

jump jump

Let's now practice filling in the missing letters to our new word below. Each word is the word 'find'. Decide which letters are missing and fill them into the spaces provided.

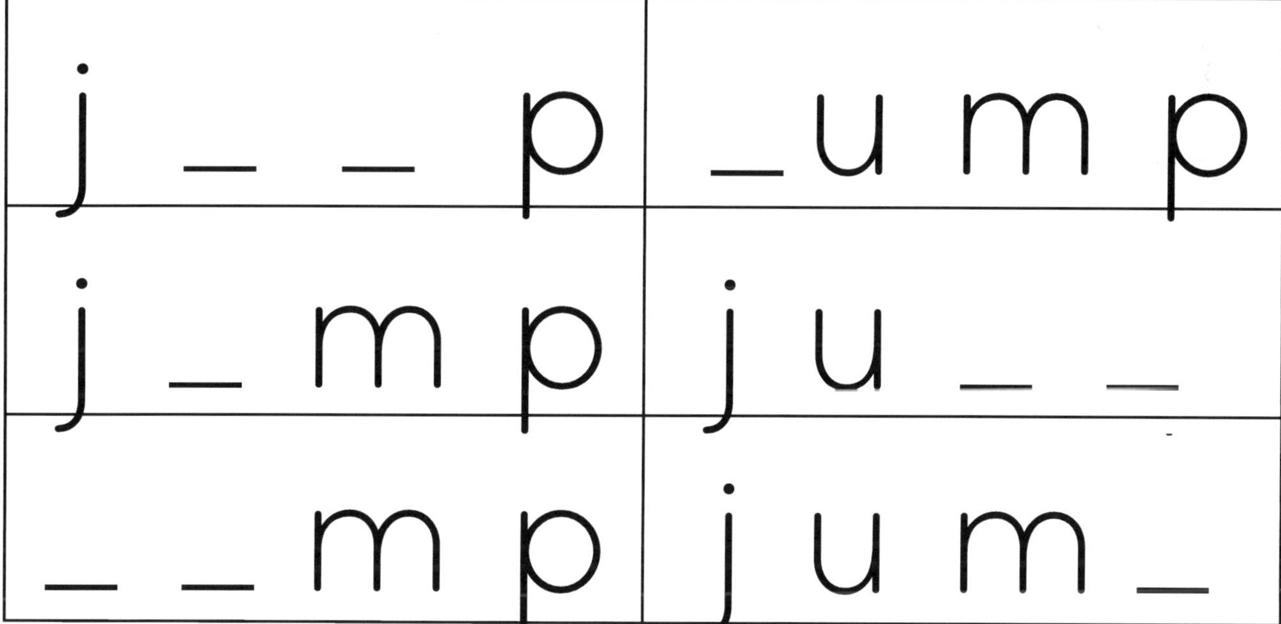

Amazing! Let's move on. The next word is little.

SAY & SPELL

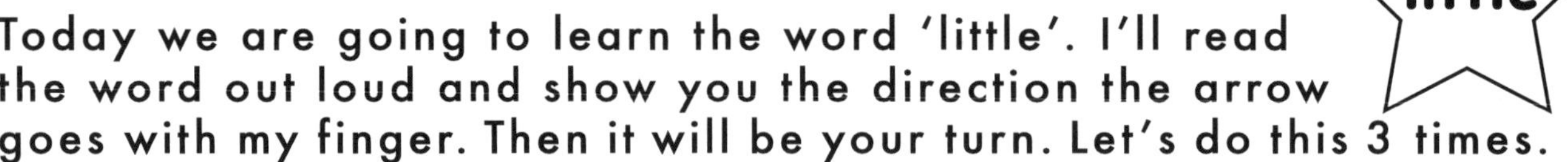

Today we are going to learn the word 'little'. I'll read the word out loud and show you the direction the arrow goes with my finger. Then it will be your turn. Let's do this 3 times.

That's great! little. I have a little sister.

Now let's learn to SPELL our new word. Say the new word out loud again but this time, spell out the letters. Let's do this 3 times.

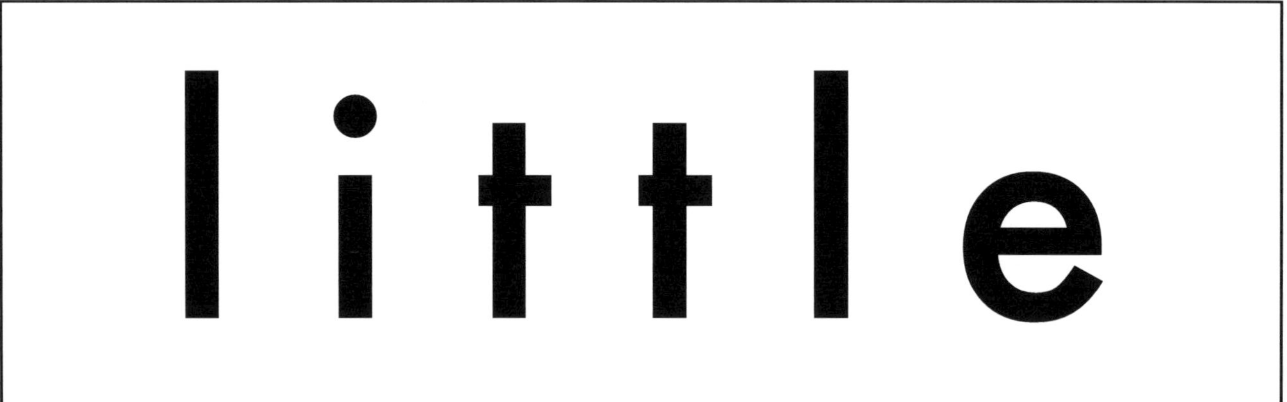

Fantastic!

Now that you can say and spell the word, let's practice tracing the letters. Using your pointer finger, trace each letter in the sky in front of you. Let's do this 3 times.

PRINT & RECOGNIZE

Now it's time to practice printing on paper. With your pencil, trace the dots and then practice on your own.

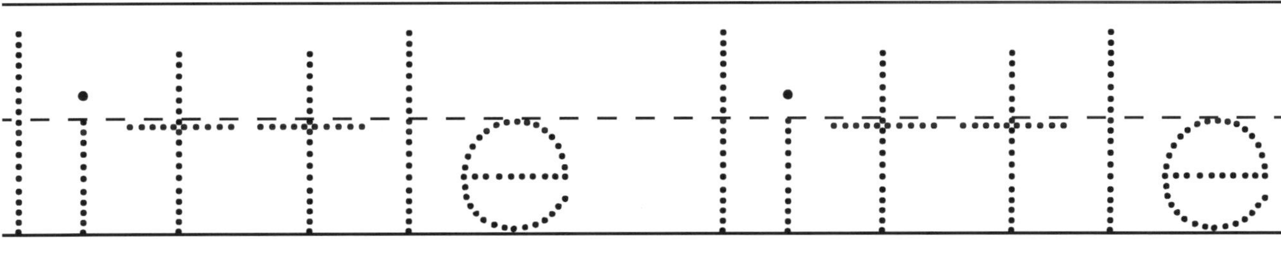

Let's see if we can recognize the words in the picture below. Color all of the birds that have the word 'little' near them. Hint: There should be 3 birds to color.

Amazing! Let's move on. The next word is look.

SAY & SPELL

look

The next word we are going to learn is 'look'. I'll read the word out loud and show you the direction the arrow goes with my finger. Then it will be your turn. Let's do this 3 times.

That's great! look. Look at the rainbow.

Now let's learn to SPELL our new word. Say the new word out loud again but this time, spell out the letters. Let's do this 3 times.

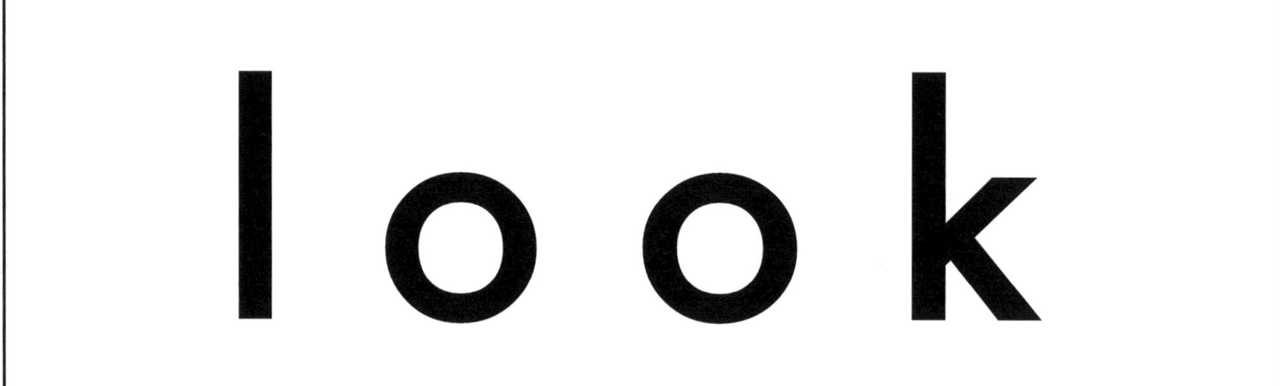

Fantastic!

Now that you can say and spell the word, let's practice tracing the letters. Using your pointer finger, trace each letter in the sky in front of you. Let's do this 3 times.

PRINT & RECOGNIZE

Now it's time to practice printing on paper. With your pencil, trace the dots and then practice on your own.

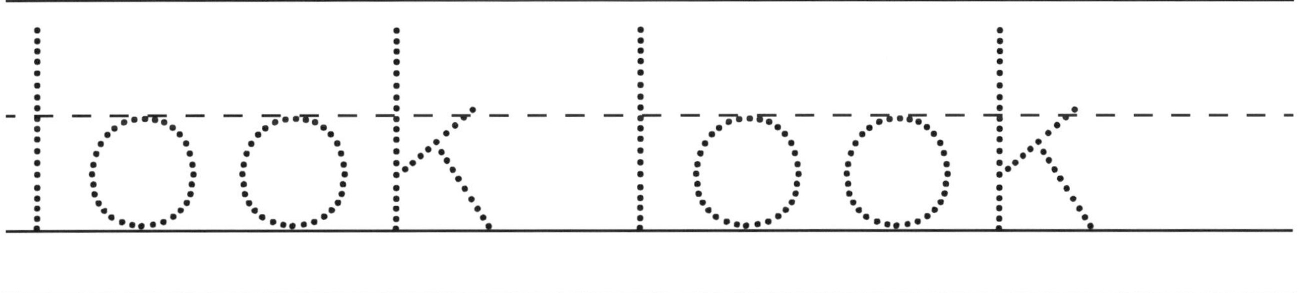

Let's see if we can recognize the words in the picture below. Circle all of the diamonds that have the word 'look' in them. Then color them all in. Hint: There are 4 diamonds to color.

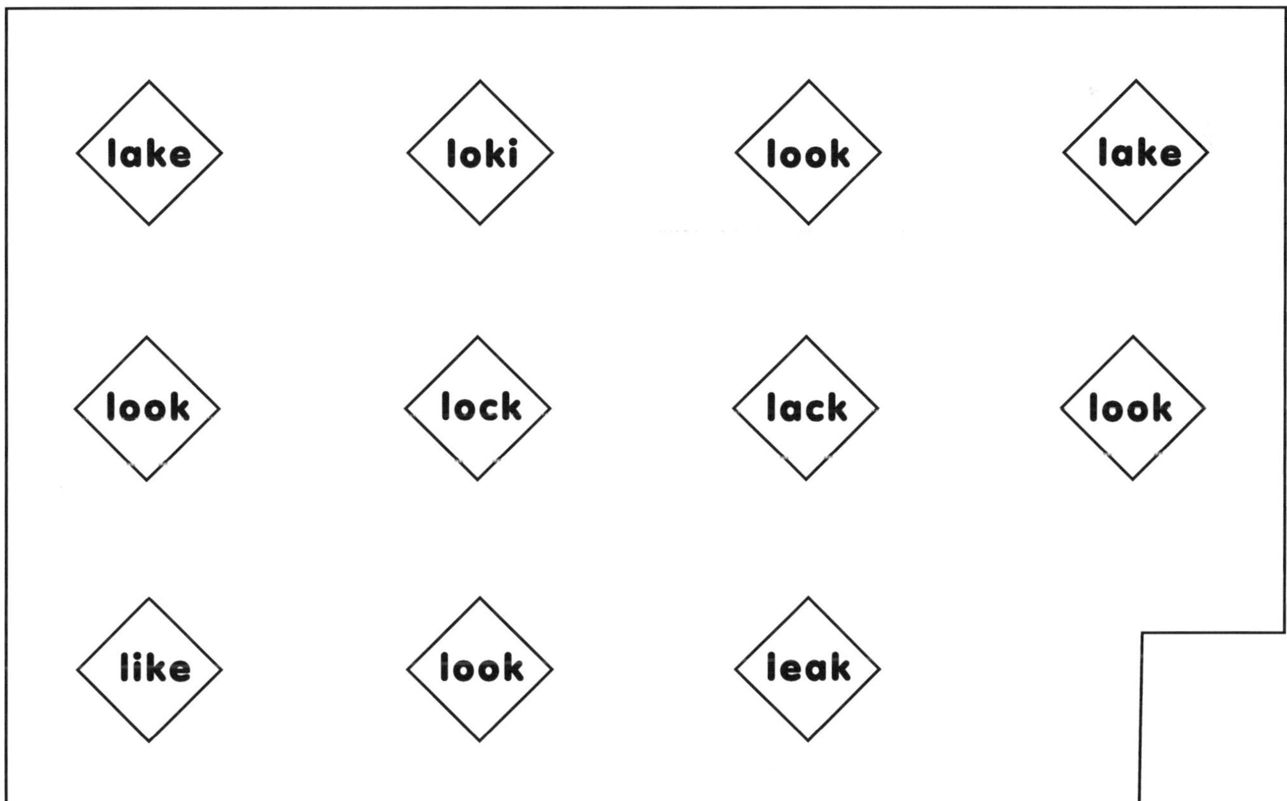

Amazing! Let's review and play a game.

FIND THE MATCHING WORD

Read the sentence and then read the list of words on the side. Find the word that best fits the sentence and then read the sentence out loud again. Pencil in the missing word in the space provided.

BATTLESHIP

Just like the boardgame, each player calls out a letter and a number to strike the other's ships. If you hit one of the letters, color in the box. If you miss, mark an x in that box. Continue until all battle ships are sunk. Tip: Place a book or a picture frame in between the boards so you can not see each other's ships.

	1	2	3	4	5	6	7
A						n	
B	o	n	e			o	
C						t	
D							
E	p	l	a	y			
F							
G							

	1	2	3	4	5	6	7
A							
B		o			n	o	t
C		n					
D		e					
E				p	l	a	y
F							
G							

SAY & SPELL

make

Today we are going to learn the word 'make'. I'll read the word out loud and show you the direction the arrow goes with my finger. Then it will be your turn. Let's do this 3 times.

That's great! make. I love to make and build new things.

Now let's learn to SPELL our new word. Say the new word out loud again but this time, spell out the letters. Let's do this 3 times.

m a k e

Fantastic!

Now that you can say and spell the word, let's practice tracing the letters. Using your pointer finger, trace each letter in the sky in front of you. Let's do this 3 times.

PRINT & RECOGNIZE

Now it's time to practice printing on paper. With your pencil, trace the dots and then practice on your own.

make make

Let's see if we can recognize the words in the picture below. Find the word 'make' in the word search below and circle the letters. Hint: The word is in the search 3 times.

w	m	c	j	m	s	g
h	a	b	m	a	k	e
f	k	g	r	k	g	x
y	e	w	r	e	n	

Amazing! Let's move on. The next word is me.

SAY & SPELL

Today we are going to learn the word me. I'll read the word out loud and show you the direction the arrow goes with my finger. Then it will be your turn. Let's do this 3 times.

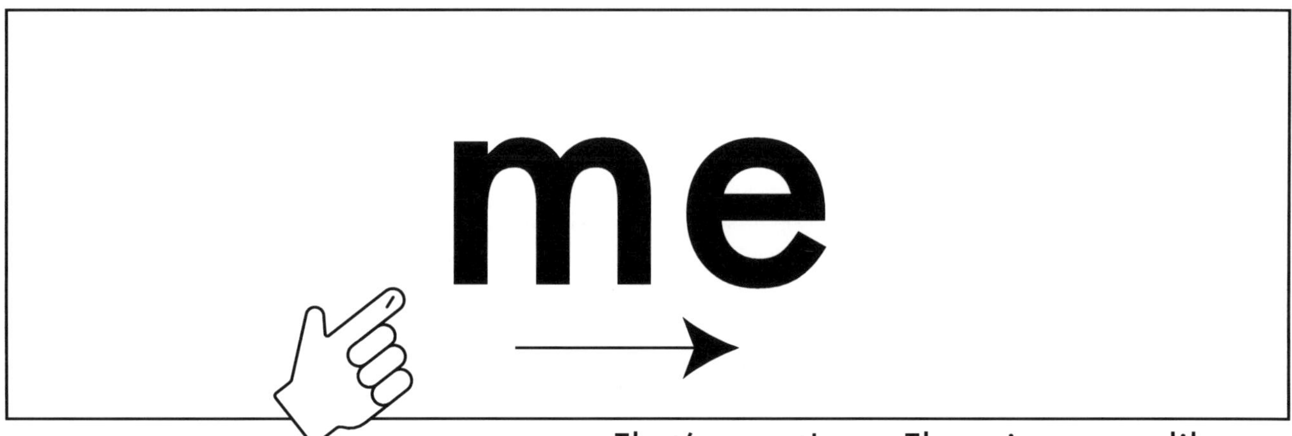

That's great! me. There is no one like me.

Now let's learn to SPELL our new word. Say the new word out loud again but this time, spell out the letters. Let's do this 3 times.

Fantastic!

Now that you can say and spell the word, let's practice tracing the letters. Using your pointer finger, trace each letter in the sky in front of you. Let's do this 3 times.

PRINT & RECOGNIZE

Now it's time to practice printing on paper. With your pencil, trace the dots and then practice on your own.

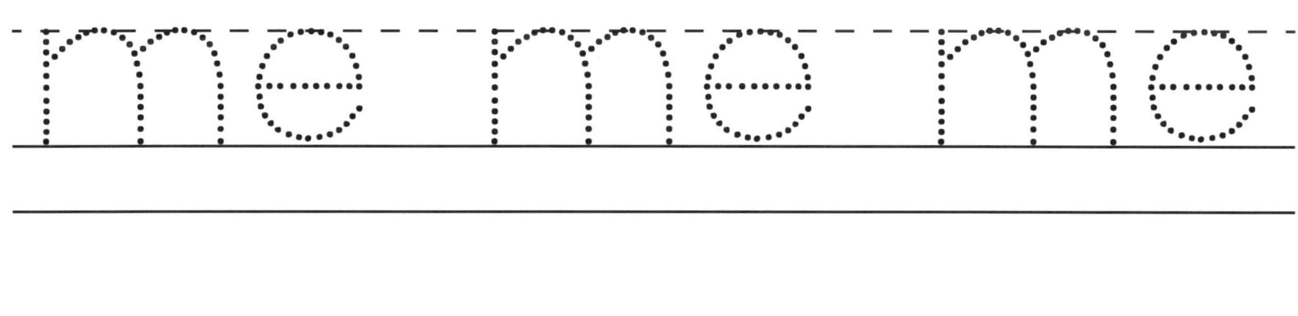

Let's figure out the animal below by connecting all of the dots with the word 'me'. Stay away from similar words as they will not help you complete the image. Hint: The image loves to eat cheese.

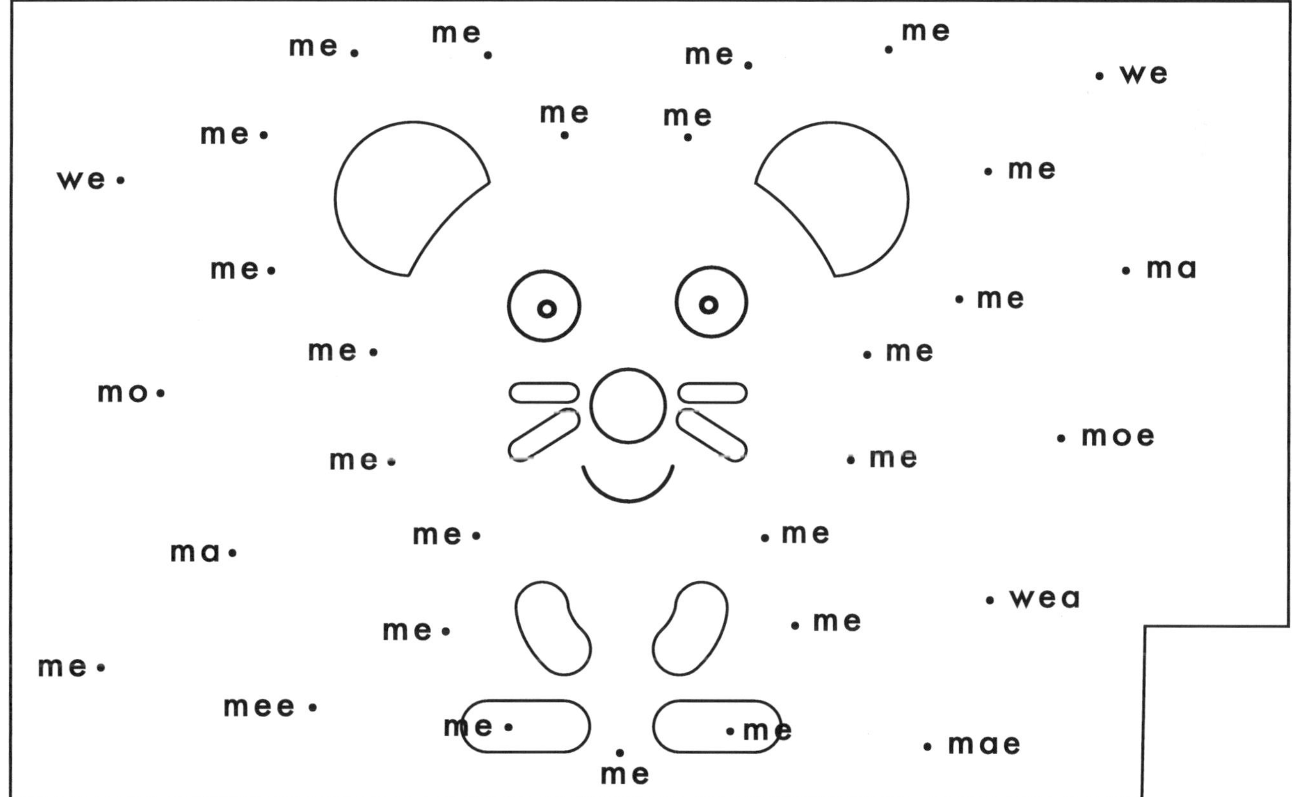

Amazing! Let's move on. The next word is my.

SAY & SPELL

my

The next word we are going to learn is 'my'. I'll read the word out loud and show you the direction the arrow goes with my finger. Then it will be your turn. Let's do this 3 times.

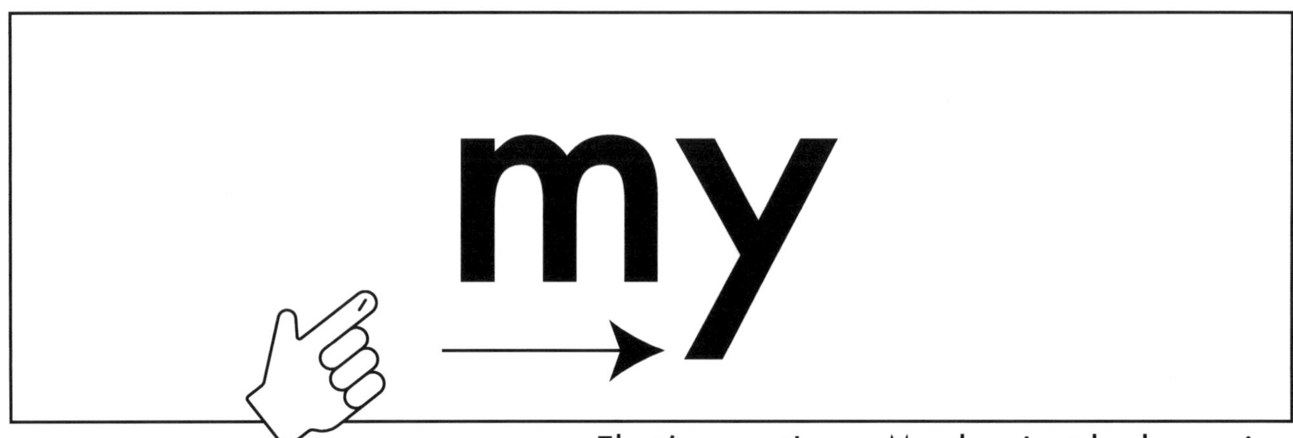

That's great! my. My dog just had puppies.

Now let's learn to SPELL our new word. Say the new word out loud again but this time, spell out the letters. Let's do this 3 times.

Fantastic!

Now that you can say and spell the word, let's practice tracing the letters. Using your pointer finger, trace each letter in the sky in front of you. Let's do this 3 times.

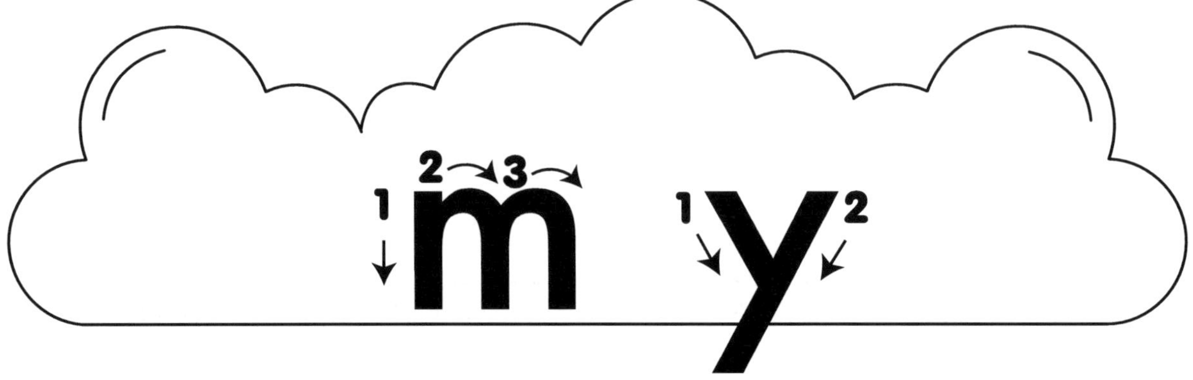

PRINT & RECOGNIZE

Now it's time to practice printing on paper. With your pencil, trace the dots and then practice on your own.

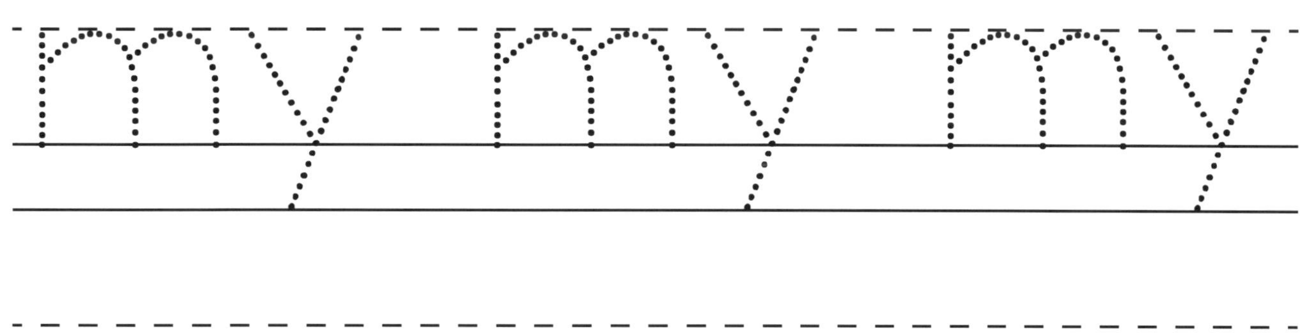

Let's see if we can recognize the words in the picture below. Match all of the different ways the word 'my' can be written by drawing a line between pairs that match.

Amazing! Let's review and play a game.

FIND THE MATCHING WORD

Read the sentences below and find the matching word from the legend. The words are in the legend twice. Circle the missing word when you find it, say it out loud and write it in the space provided.

make	me	my	make	me	my

1. I am going to ______ a pie today.

2. It will be for ______ family.

3. My mom showed ______ how.

4. I hope I ______ it well.

5. I think ____ family is going to love it.

6. They will be so proud of ____.

CREATE YOUR OWN STORY

Each player makes up one line of the story and writes it down. Fold the page over or cover the line and the next player continues. Continue until the lines are complete and then read out your funny story. The words we are practicing are highlighted in bold so you can see how they fit into the story.

1. **My** pet ________(animal)________,

2. Met a laughing ______(animal)______,

3. And they began to **make** a __(food)__,

4. The __(#1)__ added the __(ingredient)__,

5. And the __(#2)__ added the (ingredient),

6. And they gave the __(#3)__ to **me**!

SAY & SPELL

Today we are going to learn the word 'not'. I'll read the word out loud and show you the direction the arrow goes with my finger. Then it will be your turn. Let's do this 3 times.

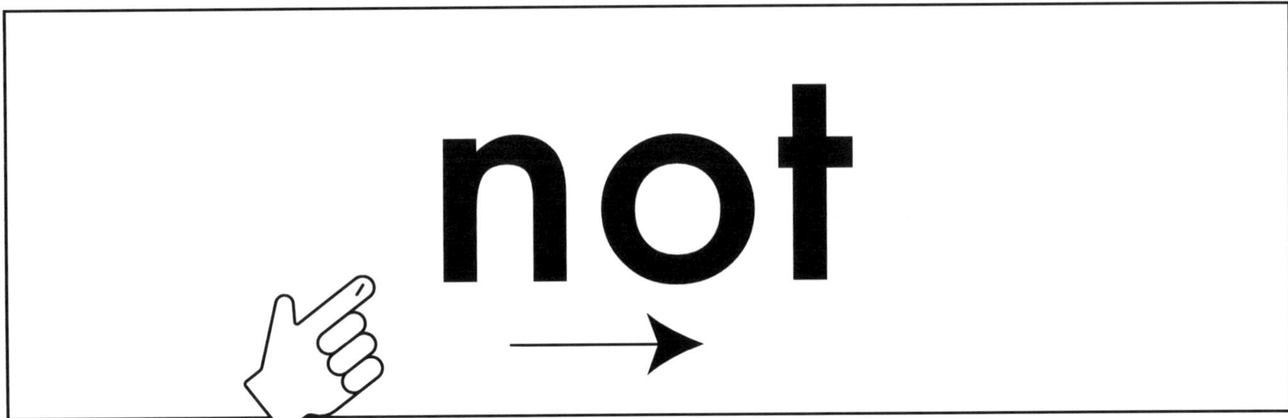

That's great! not. I am not able to come over today.

Now let's learn to SPELL our new word. Say the new word out loud again but this time, spell out the letters. Let's do this 3 times.

Fantastic!

Now that you can say and spell the word, let's practice tracing the letters. Using your pointer finger, trace each letter in the sky in front of you. Let's do this 3 times.

PRINT & RECOGNIZE

Now it's time to practice printing on paper. With your pencil, trace the dots and then practice on your own.

Let's see if we can recognize the words in the picture below. Color all of the parts of the butterfly that have the word 'not' on them. Hint: There should be 6 words to find.

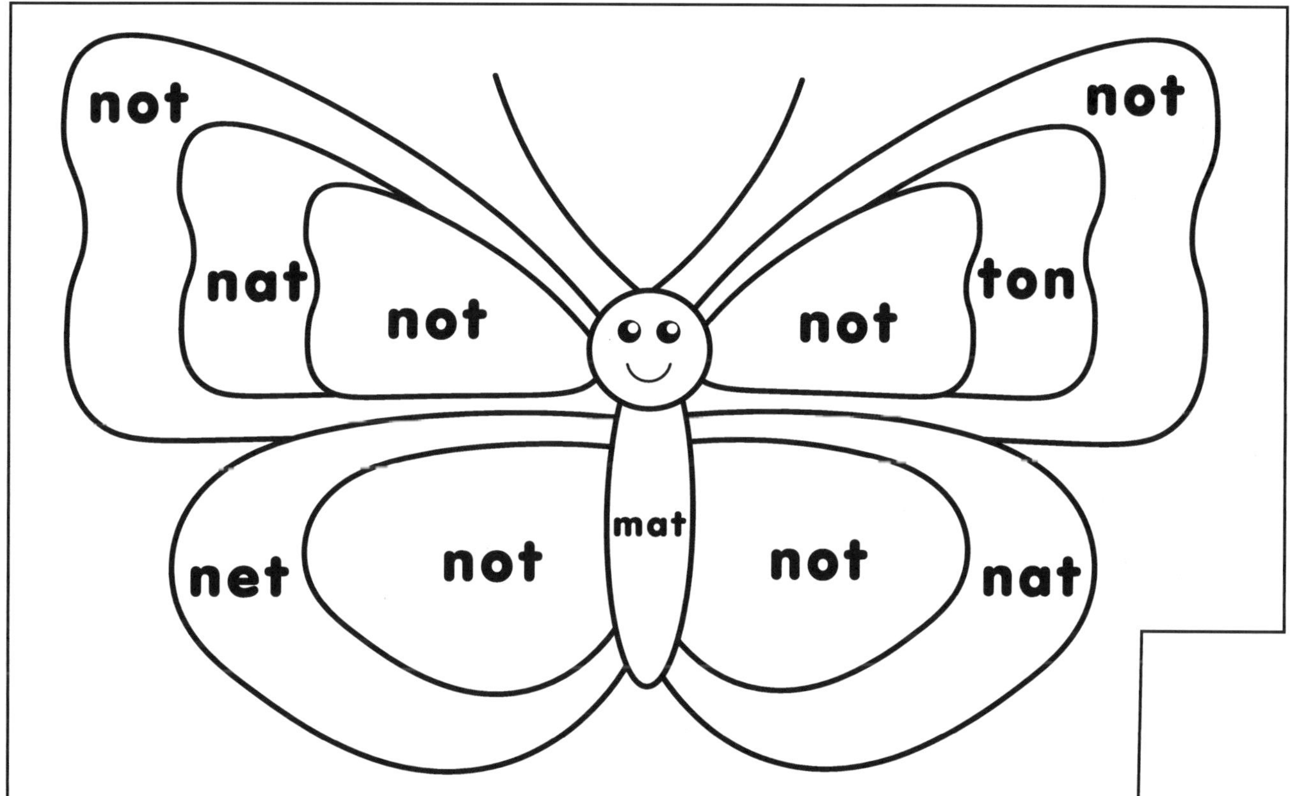

Amazing! Let's move on. The next word is one.

SAY & SPELL

one

Today we are going to learn the word 'one'. I'll read the word out loud and show you the direction the arrow goes with my finger. Then it will be your turn. Let's do this 3 times.

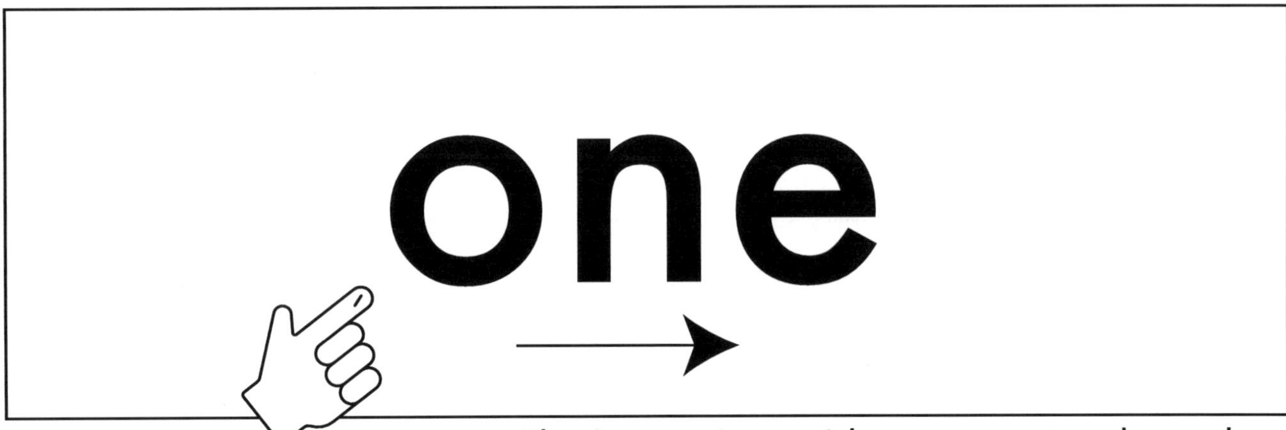

That's great! one. I have one cat and one dog.

Now let's learn to SPELL our new word. Say the new word out loud again but this time, spell out the letters. Let's do this 3 times.

Fantastic!

Now that you can say and spell the word, let's practice tracing the letters. Using your pointer finger, trace each letter in the sky in front of you. Let's do this 3 times.

PRINT & RECOGNIZE

Now it's time to practice printing on paper. With your pencil, trace the dots and then practice on your own.

one one

Let's see if we can make our way through the wilderness to school by following the word 'one'. When you come across the word, read it out loud. Beware of similar words, as they will not lead you out.

Amazing! Let's move on. The next word is play.

SAY & SPELL

The next word we are going to learn is 'play'. I'll read the word out loud and show you the direction the arrow goes with my finger. Then it will be your turn. Let's do this 3 times.

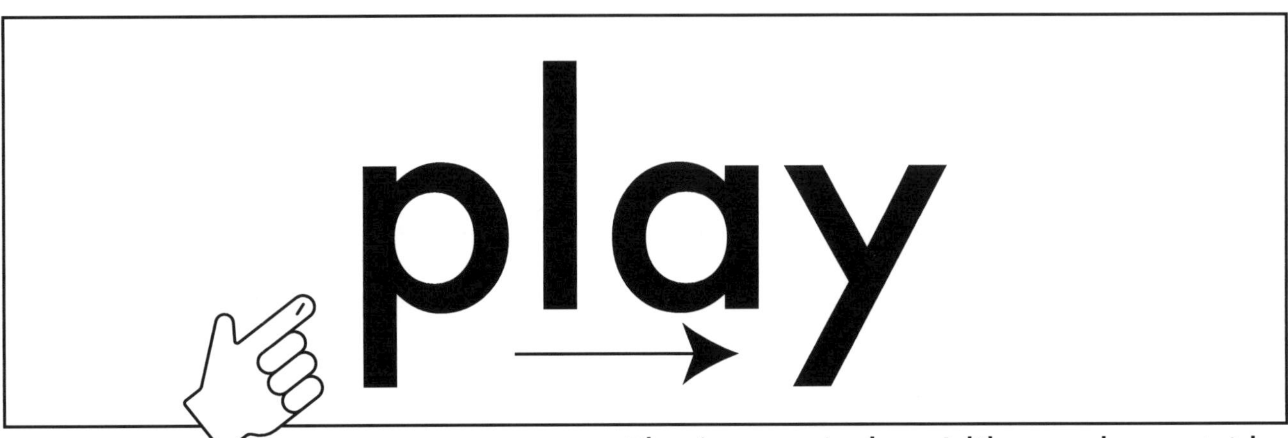

That's great! play. I like to play outside.

Now let's learn to SPELL our new word. Say the new word out loud again but this time, spell out the letters. Let's do this 3 times.

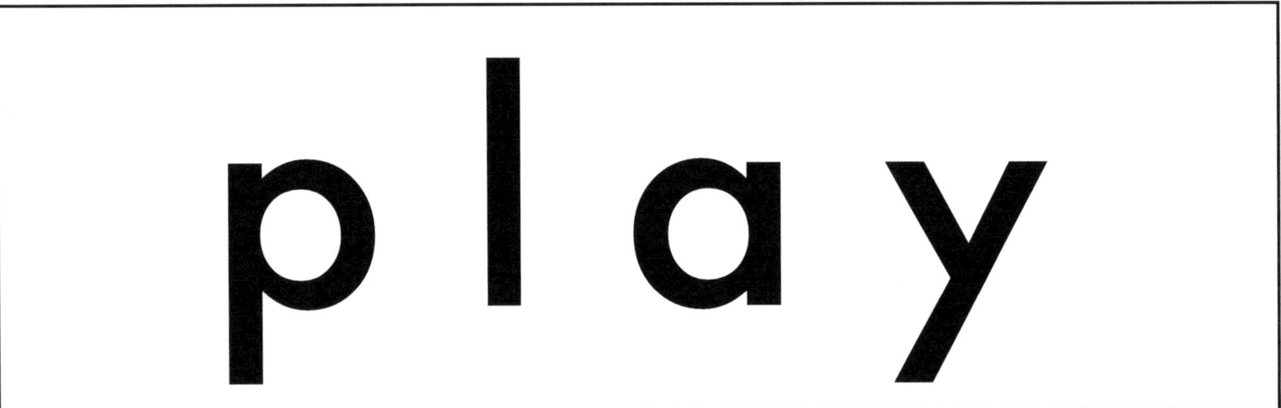

Fantastic!

Now that you can say and spell the word, let's practice tracing the letters. Using your pointer finger, trace each letter in the sky in front of you. Let's do this 3 times.

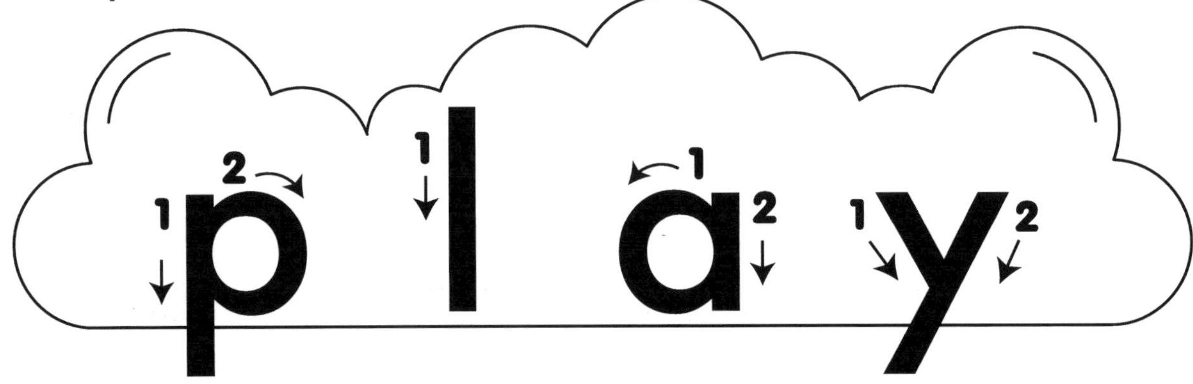

PRINT & RECOGNIZE

Now it's time to practice printing on paper. With your pencil, trace the dots and then practice on your own.

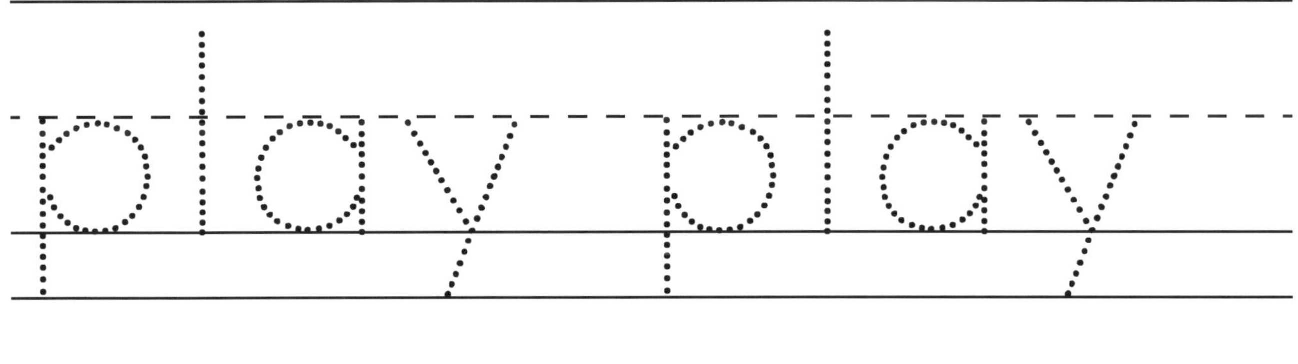

Let's see if we can figure out the missing letters in our new word below. Read the word at the bottom of the page and then pencil in the missing letters in the apples above.

Amazing! Let's review and play a game.

FIND THE MATCHING WORD

Read the sentences below and find the matching word from the list. Write in the missing word and say it out loud.

one	play	not	one	not	play

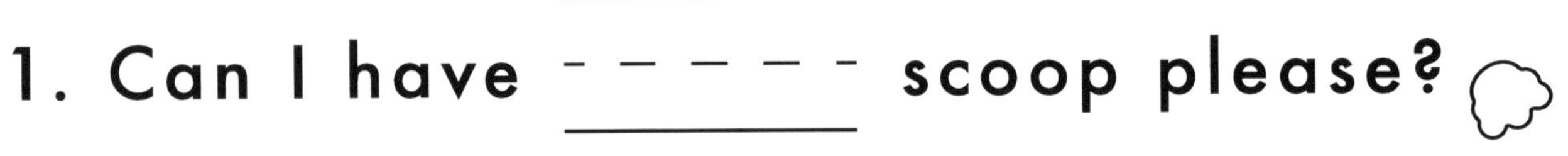

1. Can I have ______ scoop please?

2. ______ scoop of chocolate please.

3. I do ______ like vanilla.

4. After ice cream I will go ______ .

5. But ______ until I am done.

6. Then I will ______ until night time.

BUG SWAT GAME

This game is best played with 2 or more players. One adult/reader reads the word outloud and the 2+ players race to find the word on the page. The first person to swat the the bug with their hands wins the round. Continue until you have gone through all of the sight words you are practicing.

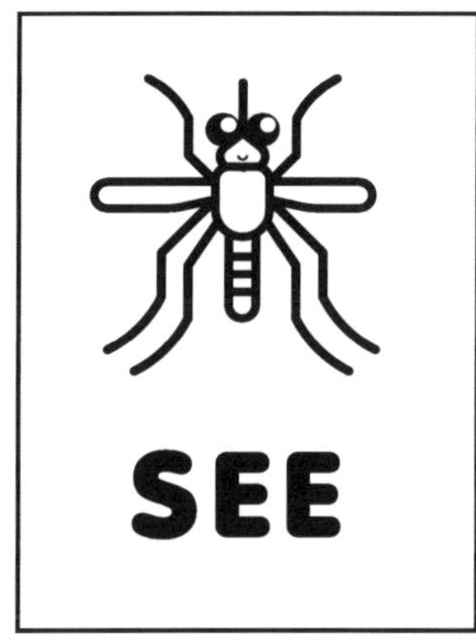

SAY & SPELL

red

Today we are going to learn the word 'red'. I'll read the word out loud and show you the direction the arrow goes with my finger. Then it will be your turn. Let's do this 3 times.

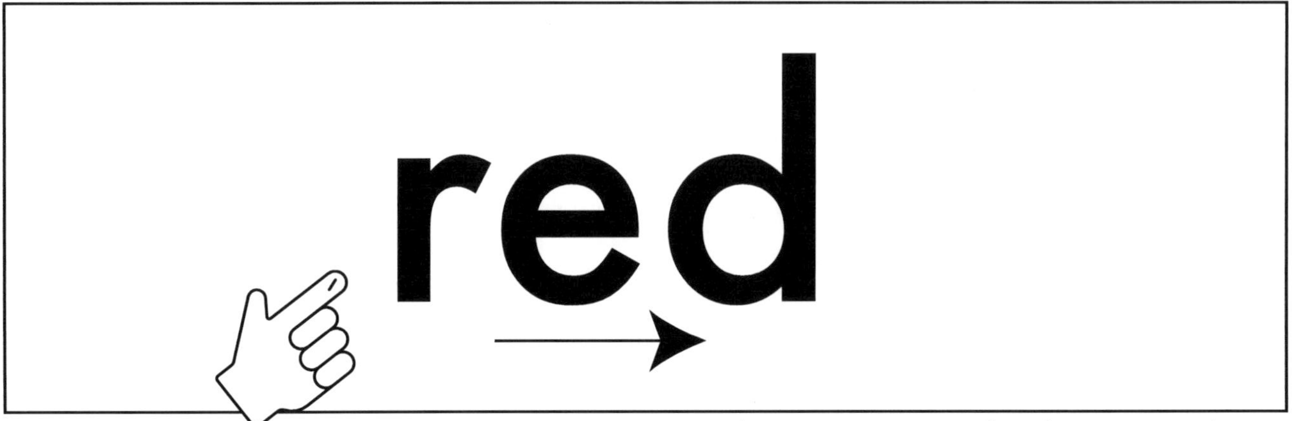

That's great! red. I have a red car.

Now let's learn to SPELL our new word. Say the new word out loud again but this time, spell out the letters. Let's do this 3 times.

Fantastic!

Now that you can say and spell the word, let's practice tracing the letters. Using your pointer finger, trace each letter in the sky in front of you. Let's do this 3 times.

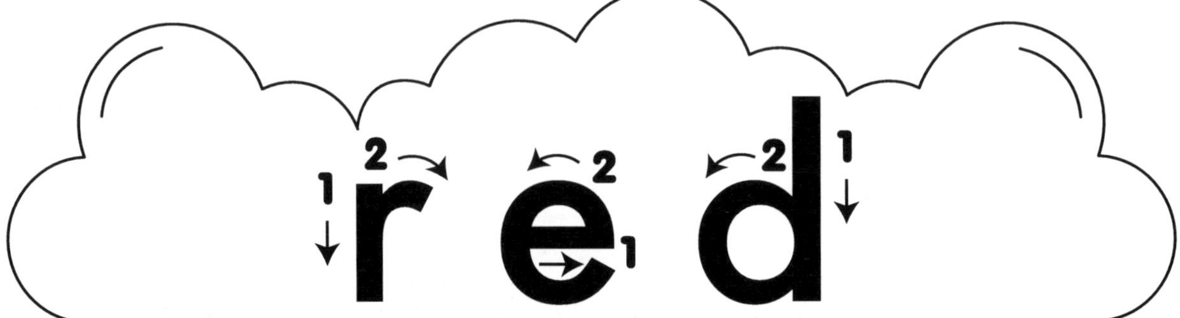

PRINT & RECOGNIZE

Now it's time to practice printing on paper. With your pencil, trace the dots and then practice on your own.

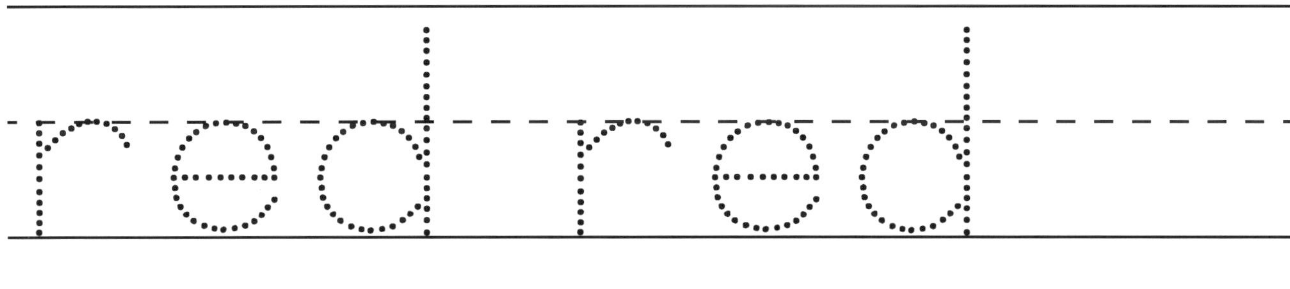

To really remember our new word, let's see if we can recognize the word among other words that look similar. Circle all of the 'red' words below. Hint: There should be 4 words to circle.

rad bred rid red
read greed
rod
raid red
reed
road
red ride red

Amazing! Let's move on. The next word is run.

SAY & SPELL

run

Today we are going to learn the word 'run'. I'll read the word out loud and show you the direction the arrow goes with my finger. Then it will be your turn. Let's do this 3 times.

That's great! run. I can run very fast.

Now let's learn to SPELL our new word. Say the new word out loud again but this time, spell out the letters. Let's do this 3 times.

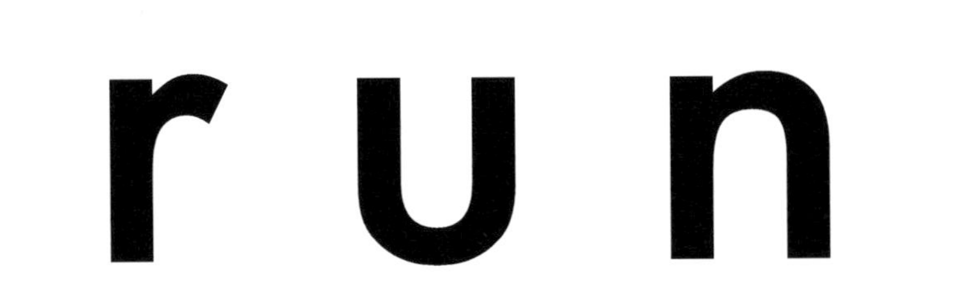

Fantastic!

Now that you can say and spell the word, let's practice tracing the letters. Using your pointer finger, trace each letter in the sky in front of you. Let's do this 3 times.

PRINT & RECOGNIZE

Now it's time to practice printing on paper. With your pencil, trace the dots and then practice on your own.

run run

Let's see if we can recognize the words in the picture below. Color all of the camping items that have the word 'run' below them. Hint: There should be 4 pictures to color.

Amazing! Let's move on. The next word is said.

SAY & SPELL

said

The next word we are going to learn is said. I'll read the word out loud and show you the direction the arrow goes with my finger. Then it will be your turn. Let's do this 3 times.

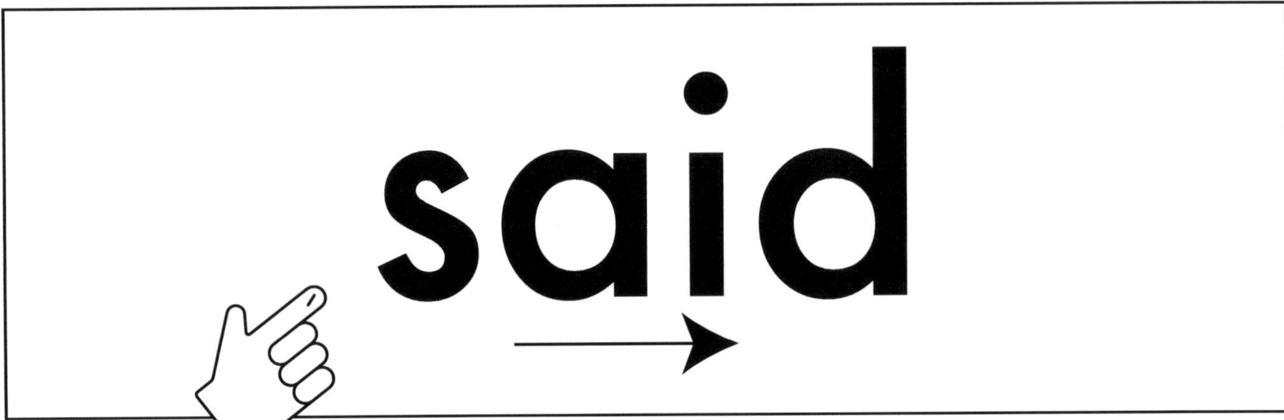

That's great! said. I said "Have a great day!".

Now let's learn to SPELL our new word. Say the new word out loud again but this time, spell out the letters. Let's do this 3 times.

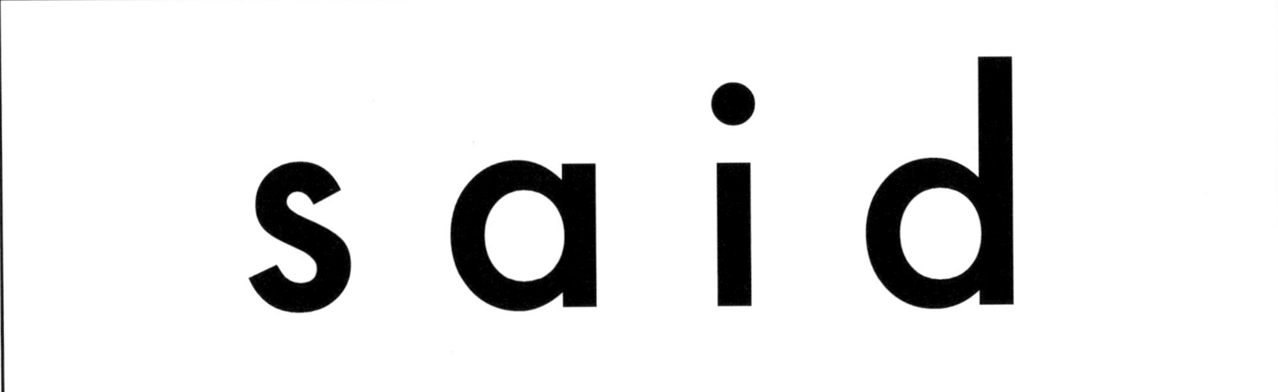

Fantastic!

Now that you can say and spell the word, let's practice tracing the letters. Using your pointer finger, trace each letter in the sky in front of you. Let's do this 3 times.

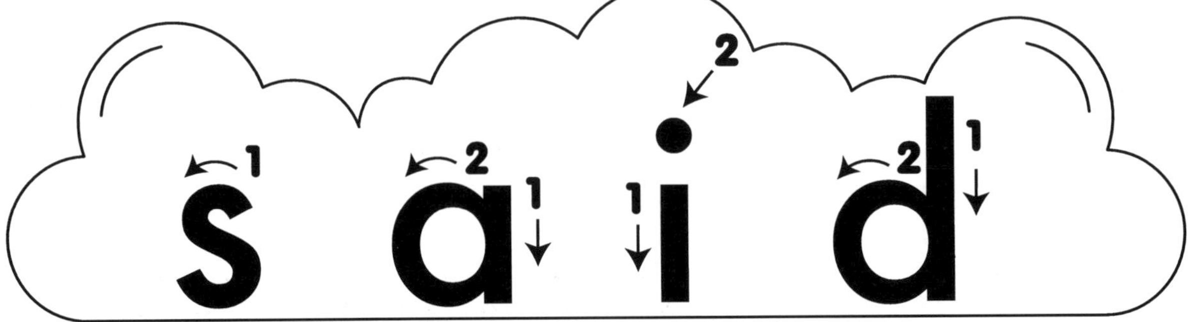

PRINT & RECOGNIZE

Now it's time to practice printing on paper. With your pencil, trace the dots and then practice on your own.

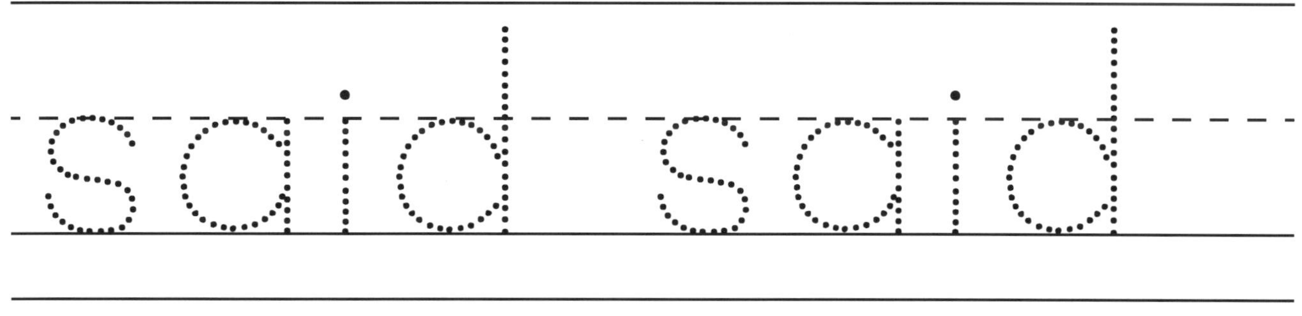

Let's see if we can recognize the words in the picture below. Circle all of the stars that have the word 'said' in them. Then color them all in. Hint: There are 3 stars to color.

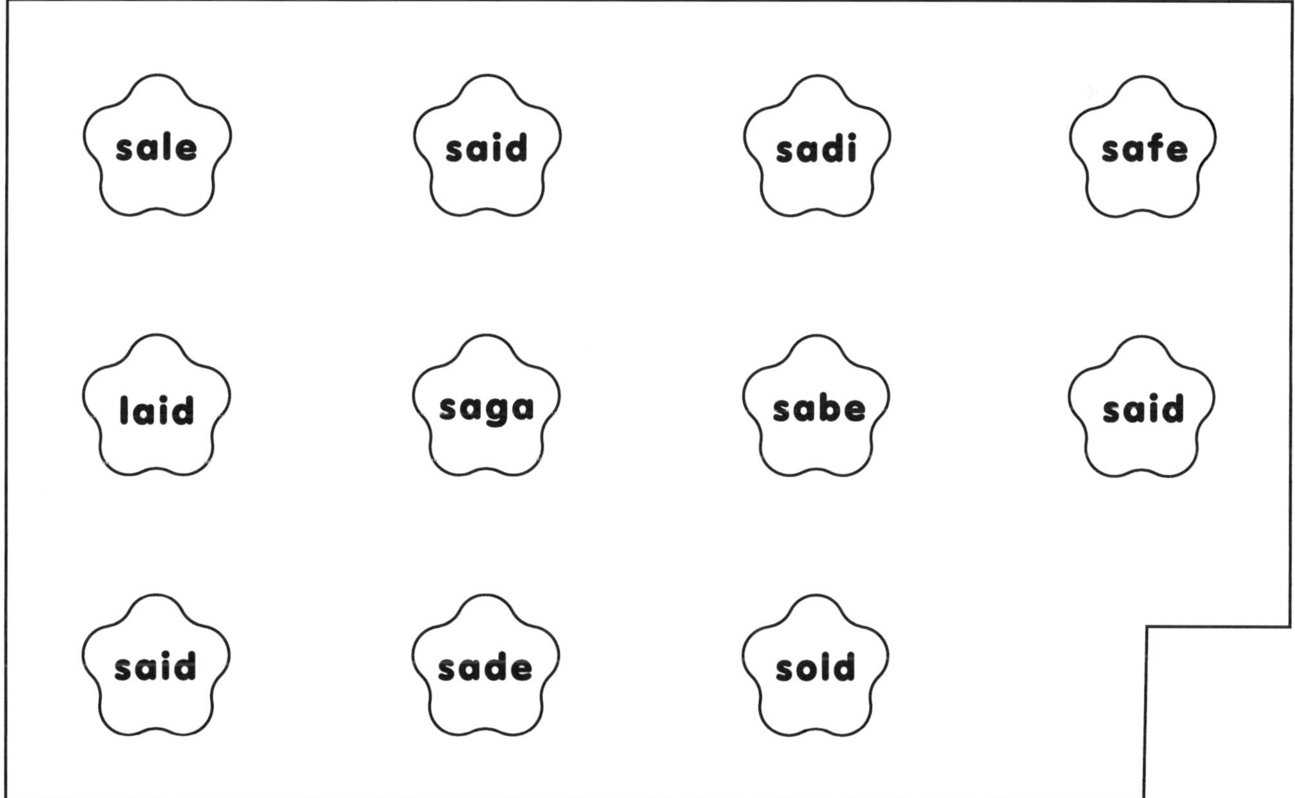

Amazing! Let's review and play a game.

READ AND DRAW

Read the words in the boxes and find the matching shape in the legend to the right. Draw the matching shapes around the words until you have completed the full chart. To make it more challenging, use the word in a different sentence each time.

run	red	said	said
red	said	red	run
run	red	red	said
said	run	red	red
red	said	red	run
red	run	said	run

Legend
◇ red
○ run
☆ said

SNAKES & LADDERS GAME

This game is played the same way as regular snakes and ladders. Take turns to roll your dice. Move a coin along the board. When you land on a word, read it out loud. If you can't read the word, skip a turn. Play until someone wins the game.

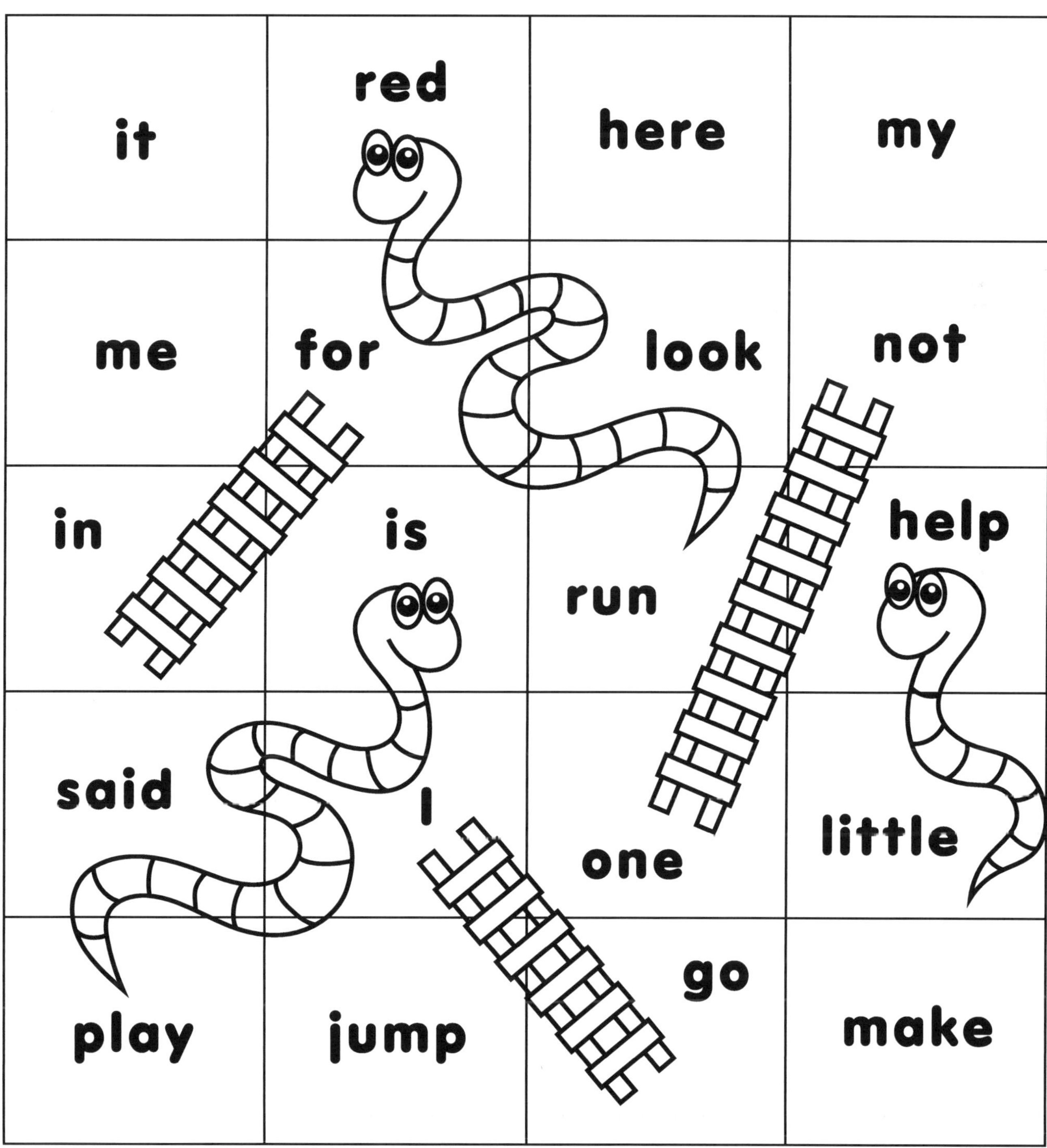

SAY & SPELL

see

Today we are going to learn the word 'see'. I'll read the word out loud and show you the direction the arrow goes with my finger. Then it will be your turn. Let's do this 3 times.

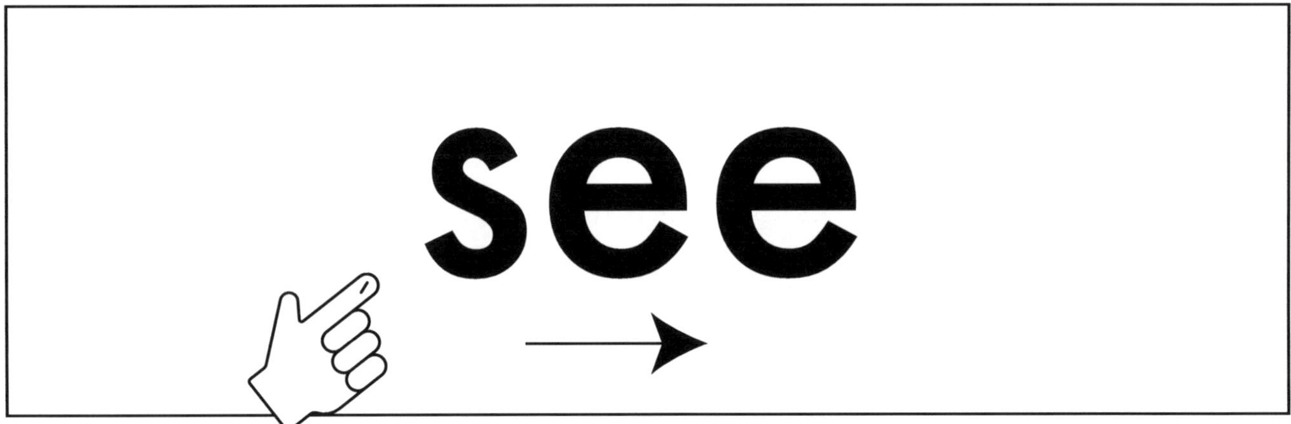

That's great! see. I can see the stars.

Now let's learn to SPELL our new word. Say the new word out loud again but this time, spell out the letters. Let's do this 3 times.

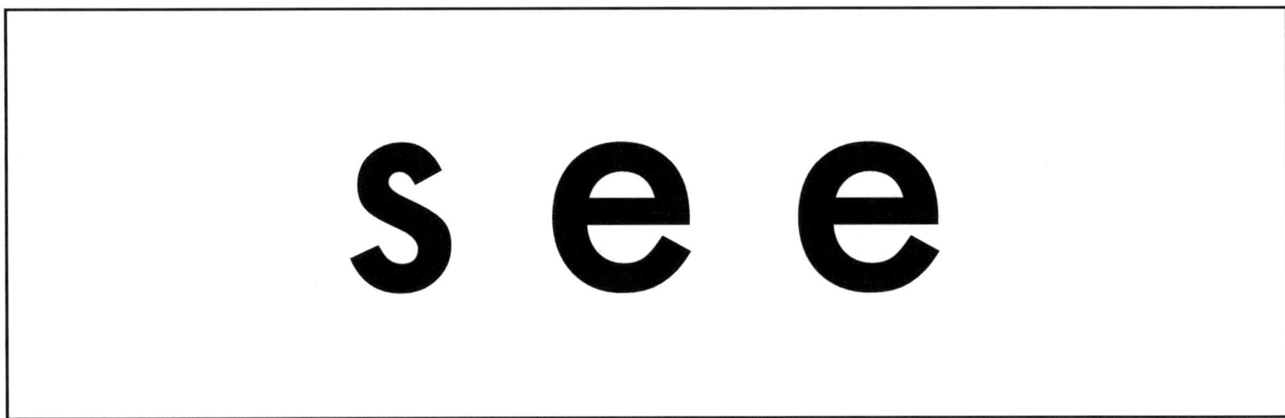

Fantastic!

Now that you can say and spell the word, let's practice tracing the letters. Using your pointer finger, trace each letter in the sky in front of you. Let's do this 3 times.

PRINT & RECOGNIZE

Now it's time to practice printing on paper. With your pencil, trace the dots and then practice on your own.

see see

To really remember our new word, let's see if we can recognize the word amongst other words that look similar. Circle all of the 'see' words below. Hint: There should be 5 words to circle.

s	e	a	o	s	u	s
e	s	e	e	e	c	e
e	t	q	s	e	e	e
v	a	e	k	e	m	

Amazing! Let's move on. The next word is the.

SAY & SPELL

Today we are going to learn the word 'the'. I'll read the word out loud and show you the direction the arrow goes with my finger. Then it will be your turn. Let's do this 3 times.

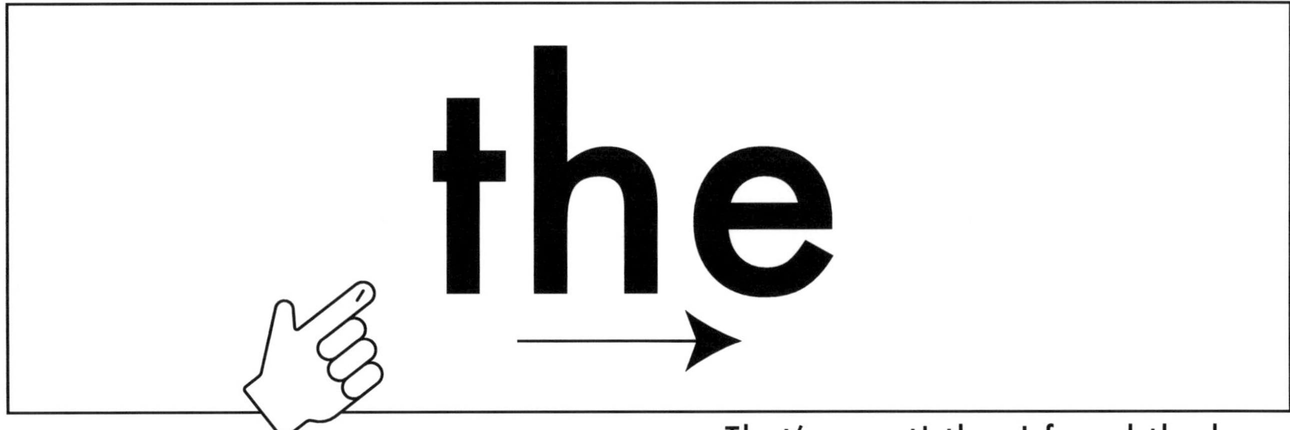

That's great! the. I found the keys.

Now let's learn to SPELL our new word. Say the new word out loud again but this time, spell out the letters. Let's do this 3 times.

Fantastic!

Now that you can say and spell the word, let's practice tracing the letters. Using your pointer finger, trace each letter in the sky in front of you. Let's do this 3 times.

PRINT & RECOGNIZE

Now it's time to practice printing on paper. With your pencil, trace the dots and then practice on your own.

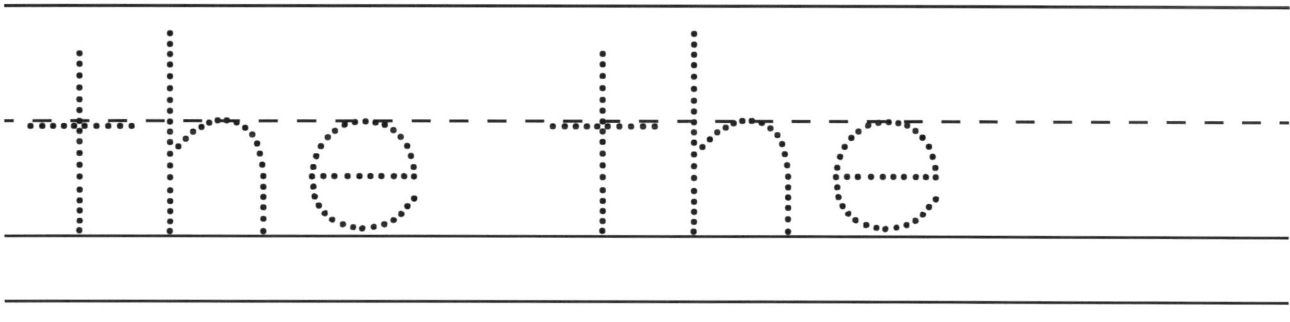

Let's complete the vehicle below by connecting all of the dots with the word 'the'. Stay away from similar words as they will not help you complete the image. Hint: The vehicle's name also is an insect.

Amazing! Let's move on. The next word is three.

SAY & SPELL

three

The next word we are going to learn is 'three'. I'll read the word out loud and show you the direction the arrow goes with my finger. Then it will be your turn. Let's do this 3 times.

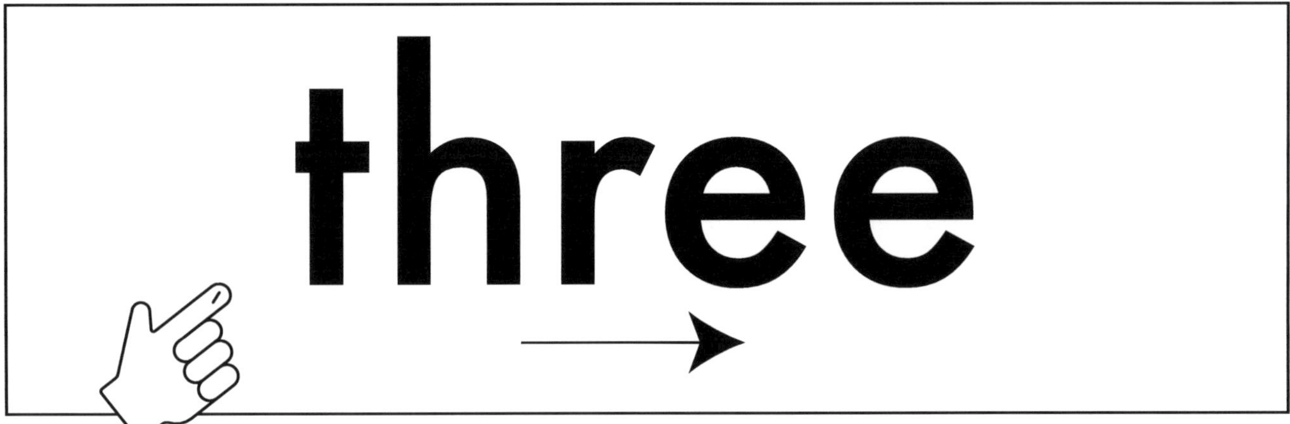

That's great! three. I am three years old.

Now let's learn to SPELL our new word. Say the new word out loud again but this time, spell out the letters. Let's do this 3 times.

t h r e e

Fantastic!

Now that you can say and spell the word, let's practice tracing the letters. Using your pointer finger, trace each letter in the sky in front of you. Let's do this 3 times.

PRINT & RECOGNIZE

Now it's time to practice printing on paper. With your pencil, trace the dots and then practice on your own.

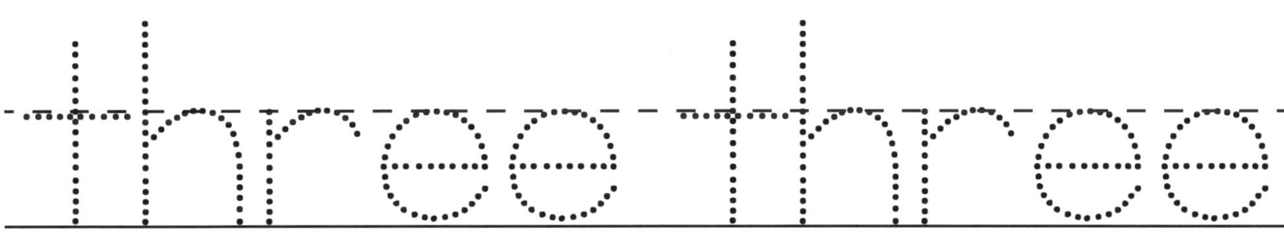

Let's see if we can recognize the words in the picture below. Match all of the different ways the word 'three' can be written by drawing a line between pairs that match.

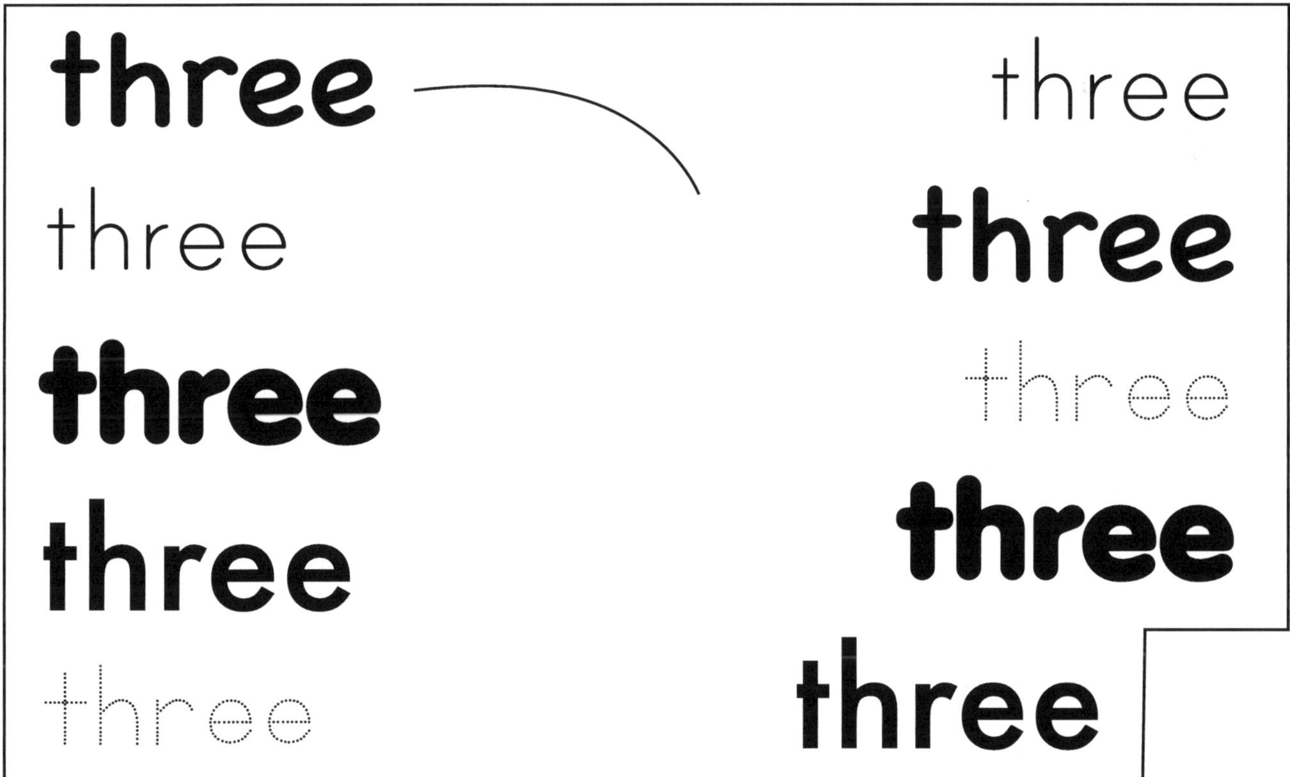

Amazing! Let's review and play a game.

BUBBLE GUM MACHINE

Match the words on the bubble gum balls to the words in the legend. Read the word out loud and use it in a sentence. Color the bubble gum balls in the colors from the legend to fill up your candy machine.

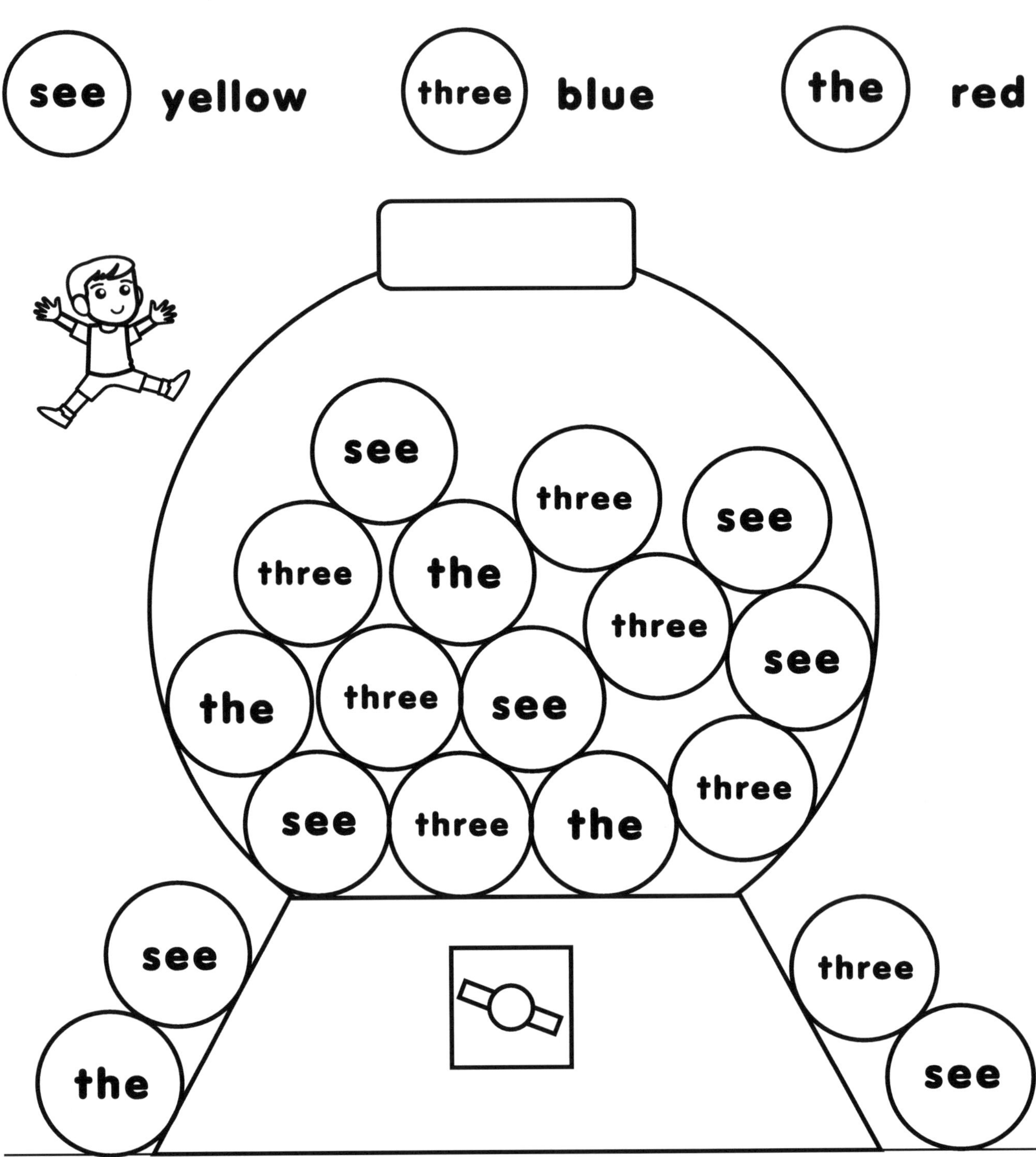

THE DOT GAME

This game is played by drawing a line connecting 2 dots. Players take turns drawing a line until they have completed drawing a box. After a box is made. they can write a word in the box. The first person to draw 3 boxes and write the 3 words below wins.

see	three	the

SAY & SPELL

to

Today we are going to learn the word 'to'. I'll read the word out loud and show you the direction the arrow goes with my finger. Then it will be your turn. Let's do this 3 times.

That's great! to. I am going to the store.

Now let's learn to SPELL our new word. Say the new word out loud again but this time, spell out the letters. Let's do this 3 times.

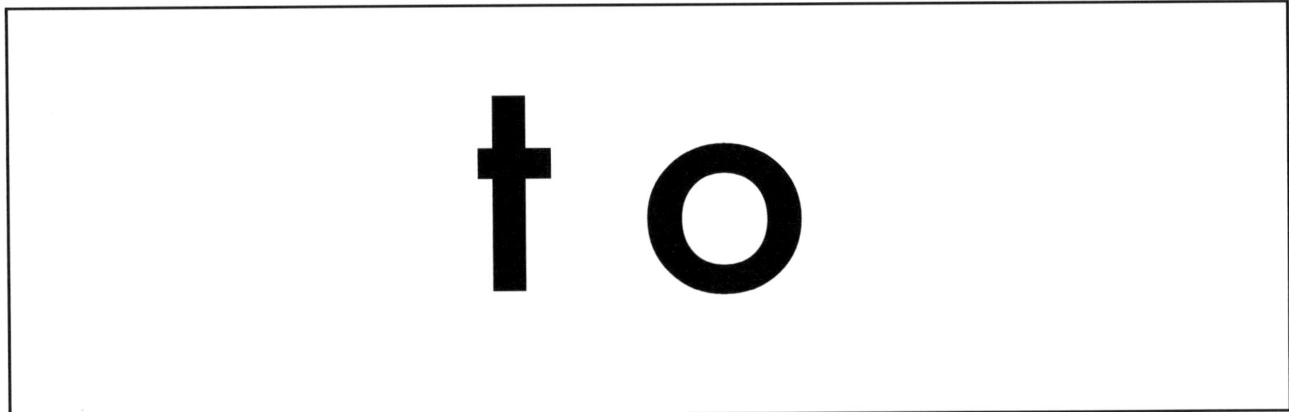

Fantastic!

Now that you can say and spell the word, let's practice tracing the letters. Using your pointer finger, trace each letter in the sky in front of you. Let's do this 3 times.

PRINT & RECOGNIZE

Now it's time to practice printing on paper. With your pencil, trace the dots and then practice on your own.

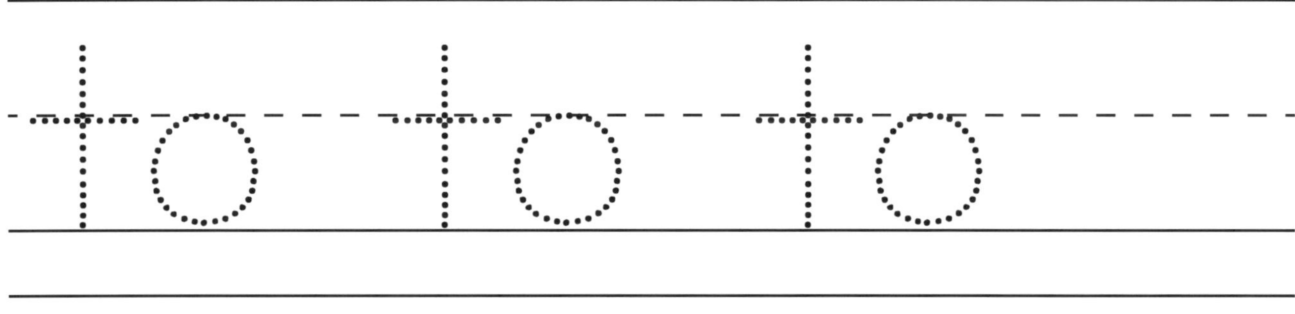

Let's see if we can spot the difference between our new word 'to' and similar words below. Color in the unicorn picture by matching the colors in the index below to the words in the picture.

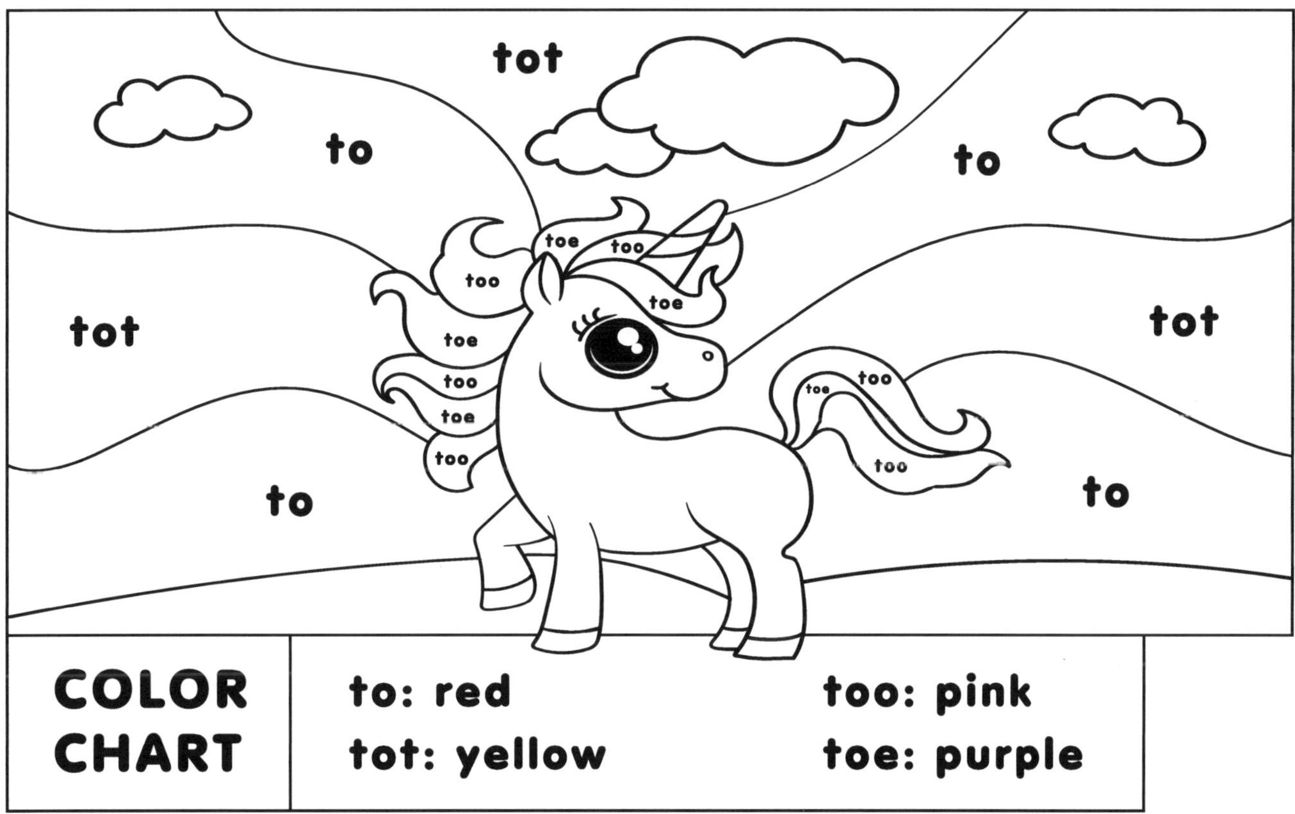

COLOR CHART	to: red tot: yellow	too: pink toe: purple

Amazing! Let's move on. The next word is two.

SAY & SPELL

Today we are going to learn the word 'two'. I'll read the word out loud and show you the direction the arrow goes with my finger. Then it will be your turn. Let's do this 3 times.

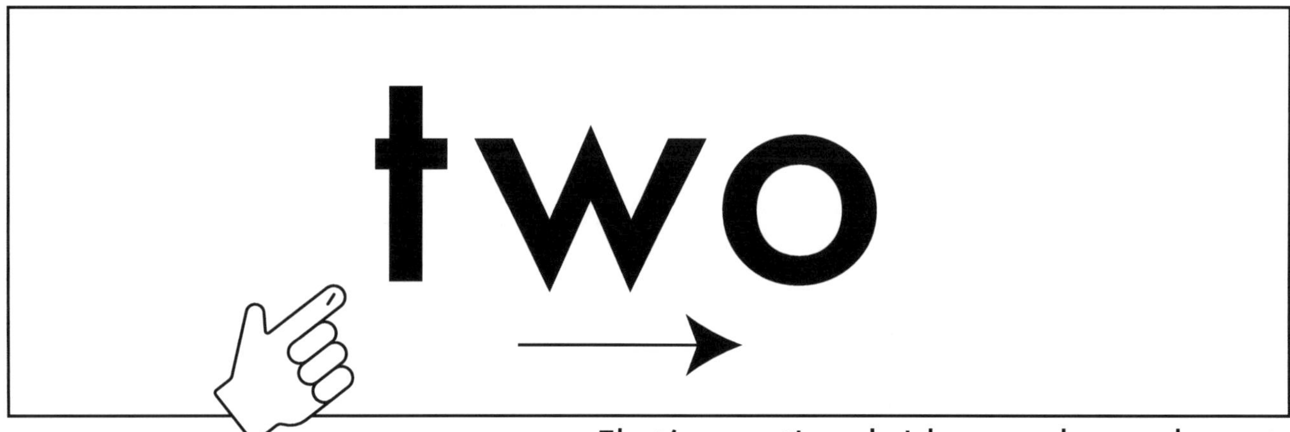

That's great! and. I have a dog and a cat.

Now let's learn to SPELL our new word. Say the new word out loud again but this time, spell out the letters. Let's do this 3 times.

Fantastic!

Now that you can say and spell the word, let's practice tracing the letters. Using your pointer finger, trace each letter in the sky in front of you. Let's do this 3 times.

PRINT & RECOGNIZE

Now it's time to practice printing on paper. With your pencil, trace the dots and then practice on your own.

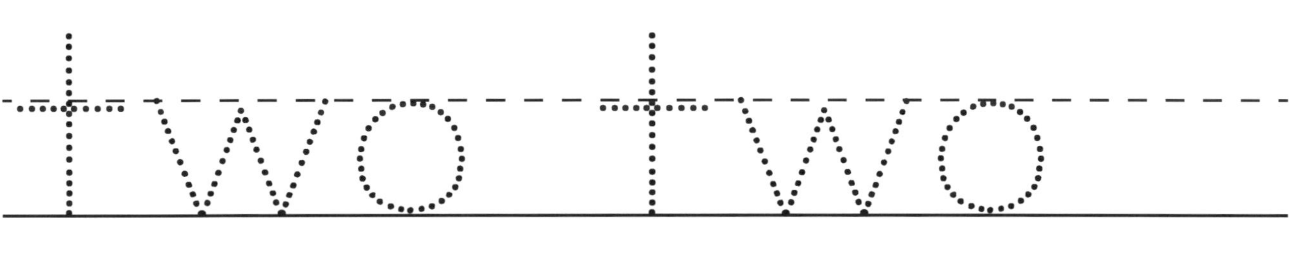

Let's see if we can make it to the center of the maze by following the word 'is'. When you come across the word, read it out loud. Beware of similar words, as they will not lead you to the center.

Amazing! Let's move on. The next word is up.

SAY & SPELL

The next word we are going to learn is 'up'. I'll read the word out loud and show you the direction the arrow goes with my finger. Then it will be your turn. Let's do this 3 times.

up

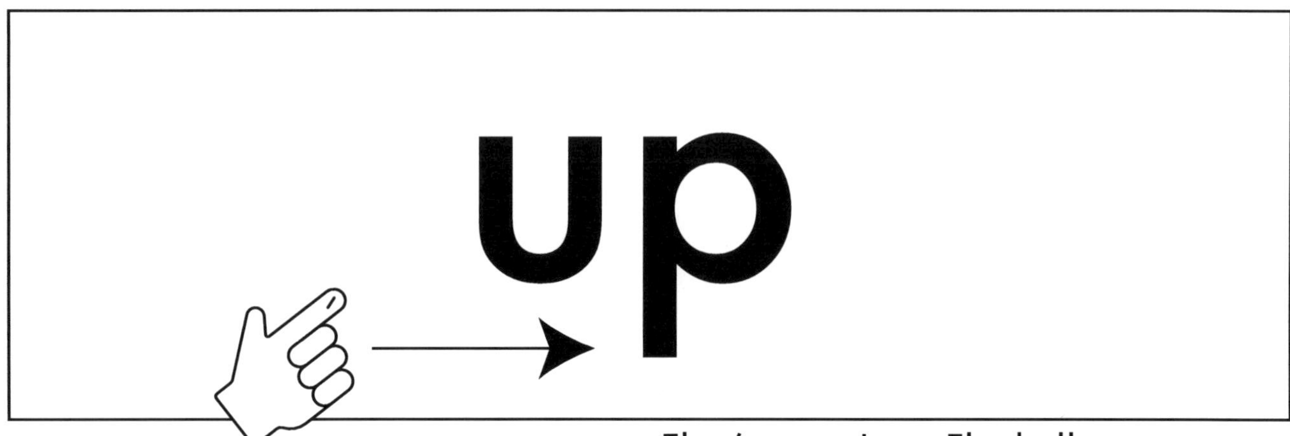

That's great! up. The balloon went up.

Now let's learn to SPELL our new word. Say the new word out loud again but this time, spell out the letters. Let's do this 3 times.

Fantastic!

Now that you can say and spell the word, let's practice tracing the letters. Using your pointer finger, trace each letter in the sky in front of you. Let's do this 3 times.

PRINT & RECOGNIZE

Now it's time to practice printing on paper. With your pencil, trace the dots and then practice on your own.

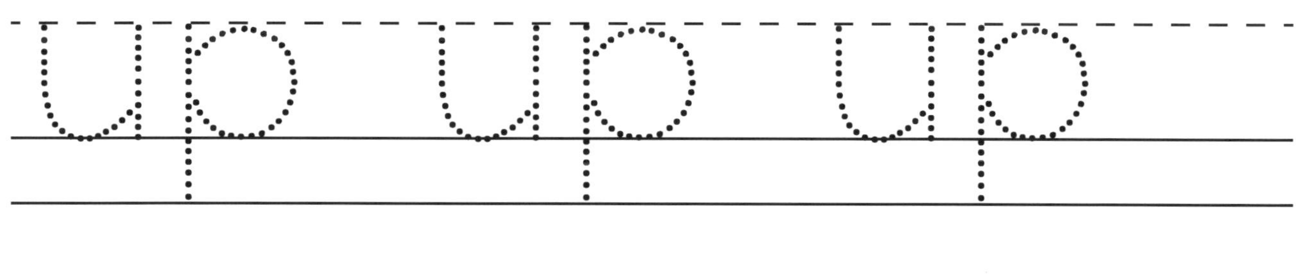

Let's see if we can recognize the words in the pictures below. Color all of the vehicles that have the word 'up' beside them. Hint: There should be 3 vehicles to color.

Amazing! Let's review and play a game.

BATTLESHIP

Just like the boardgame, each player calls out a letter and a number to strike the other's ships. If you hit one of the letters, color in the box. If you miss, mark an x in that box. Continue until all battle ships are sunk. Tip: Place a book or a picture frame in between the boards so you can not see each other's ships.

	1	2	3	4	5	6	7
A			t				
B			w			t	o
C			o				
D							
E					u	p	
F							
G							

	1	2	3	4	5	6	7
A							
B	t	o					
C							
D							
E			u	p			t
F							w
G							o

SIGHT WORD BOARD GAME

Roll the dice to see which word you land on. When you land on that word, say the word out loud, and try to use it in a sentence. Keep going until the first person makes it to the end as the winner!

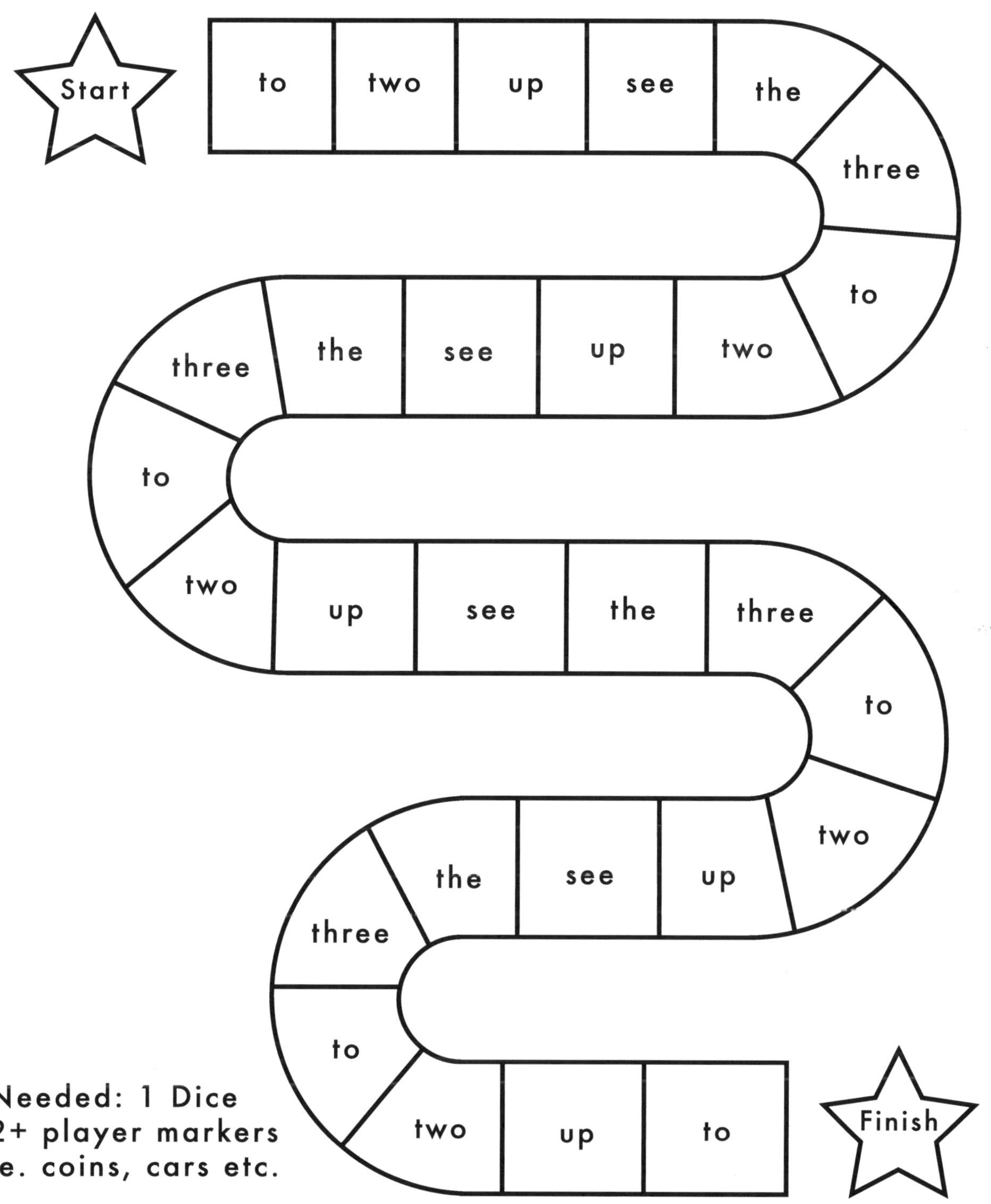

Needed: 1 Dice
2+ player markers
ie. coins, cars etc.

SAY & SPELL

Today we are going to learn the word 'we'. I'll read the word out loud and show you the direction the arrow goes with my finger. Then it will be your turn. Let's do this 3 times.

That's great! we. We are having a great time!

Now let's learn to SPELL our new word. Say the new word out loud again but this time, spell out the letters. Let's do this 3 times.

Fantastic!

Now that you can say and spell the word, let's practice tracing the letters. Using your pointer finger, trace each letter in the sky in front of you. Let's do this 3 times.

PRINT & RECOGNIZE

Now it's time to practice printing on paper. With your pencil, trace the dots and then practice on your own.

we we we

To really remember our new word, let's see if we can recognize the word among other words that look similar. Find the 4 words that don't belong and write them in the spaces provided below.

we	ew	we	we	awe
we	ewe	we	we	we
we	we	owe	we	we

Amazing! Let's move on. The next word is where.

SAY & SPELL

Today we are going to learn the word 'where'. I'll read the word out loud and show you the direction the arrow goes with my finger. Then it will be your turn. Let's do this 3 times.

where

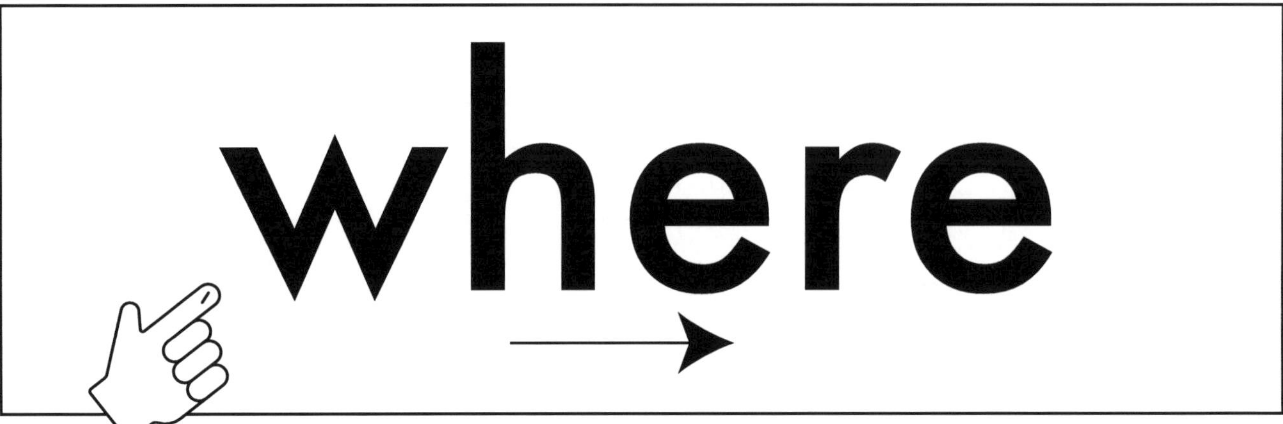

That's great! where. Where is the ice cream?

Now let's learn to SPELL our new word. Say the new word out loud again but this time, spell out the letters. Let's do this 3 times.

Fantastic!

Now that you can say and spell the word, let's practice tracing the letters. Using your pointer finger, trace each letter in the sky in front of you. Let's do this 3 times.

PRINT & RECOGNIZE

Now it's time to practice printing on paper. With your pencil, trace the dots and then practice on your own.

where where

Let's now practice filling in the missing letters to our new word below. Each word is the word 'where'. Decide which letters are missing and fill them into the spaces provided.

w_ _re	_here
w_ere	wh_ _e
_ _ere	wher_

Amazing! Let's move on. The next word is yellow.

SAY & SPELL

yellow

The next word we are going to learn is 'yellow'. I'll read the word out loud and show you the direction the arrow goes with my finger. Then it will be your turn. Let's do this 3 times.

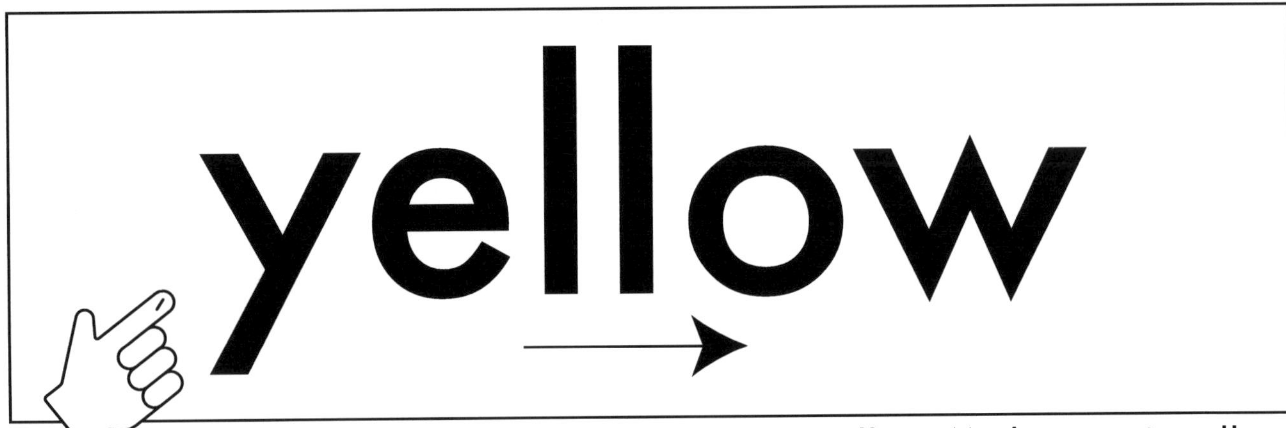

That's great! yellow. My banana is yellow.

Now let's learn to SPELL our new word. Say the new word out loud again but this time, spell out the letters. Let's do this 3 times.

Fantastic!

Now that you can say and spell the word, let's practice tracing the letters. Using your pointer finger, trace each letter in the sky in front of you. Let's do this 3 times.

PRINT & RECOGNIZE

Now it's time to practice printing on paper. With your pencil, trace the dots and then practice on your own.

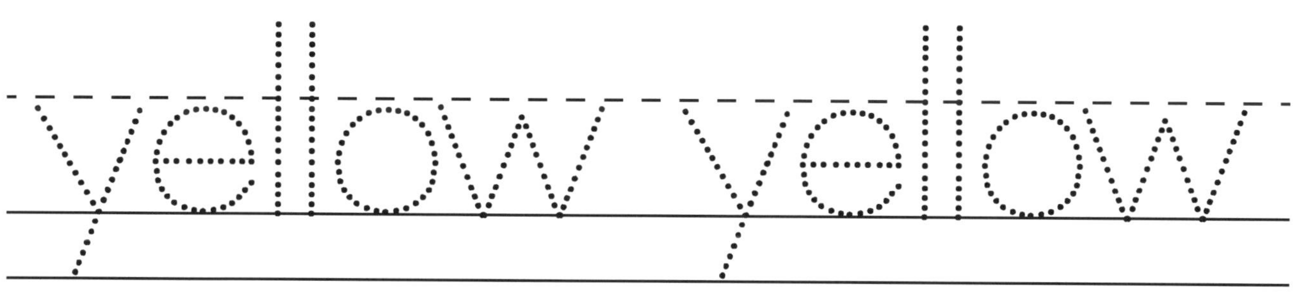

Let's see if we can recognize the words in the picture below. Circle all of the trucks that have the word 'yellow' in them. Then color them all in. Hint: There are 3 trucks to color.

Amazing! Let's review and play a game.

MONSTER PIXEL ART

Match the words in the squares to the colors in the legend to create a pixel monster. Read the words out loud and try to use them in a sentence about the monster.

COLOR CHART	yellow: yellow we: black where: pink

yellow	yellow	yellow	yellow	yellow	yellow	yellow	yellow	yellow	yellow
where	where	where	where	yellow	yellow	where	where	where	where
where				where	where				where
where		we		where	where		we		where
where				where	where				where
yellow	where	we	where	where	where	where	we	where	yellow
yellow	yellow	where	we	we	we	we	where	yellow	yellow
yellow	yellow	yellow	where	where	where	where	yellow	yellow	yellow
yellow	yellow	yellow	yellow	where	where	yellow	yellow	yellow	yellow
yellow	yellow	yellow	yellow	where	where	yellow	yellow	yellow	yellow

SPIDER WEB GAME

Using the same rules as hangman, one person chooses a word and writes it on a hidden piece of paper. They then write a line for each letter the word has. The next person has to guess the letters of the word. If you get a letter right, write it in where the letter would go. If you guess an incorrect letter, draw one part of the spider onto the web until you have either guessed the word correctly or drawn all parts of the spider. It is then the next person's turn.

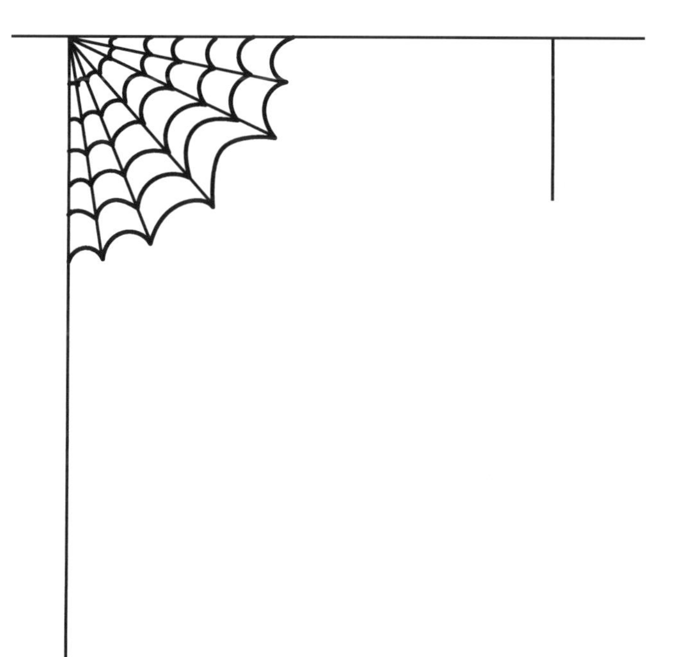

a b c d e f g h i j
k l m n o p q r s
t u v w x y z

______ ______ ______ ______ ______ ______

SAY & SPELL

Today we are going to learn the word 'you'. I'll read the word out loud and show you the direction the arrow goes with my finger. Then it will be your turn. Let's do this 3 times.

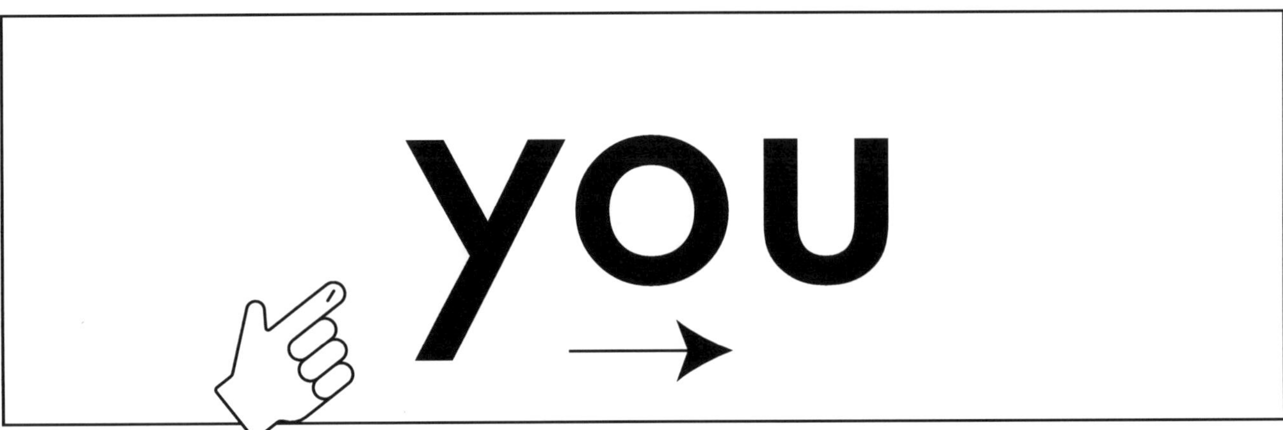

That's great! you. You are a great friend.

Now let's learn to SPELL our new word. Say the new word out loud again but this time, spell out the letters. Let's do this 3 times.

Fantastic!

Now that you can say and spell the word, let's practice tracing the letters. Using your pointer finger, trace each letter in the sky in front of you. Let's do this 3 times.

PRINT & RECOGNIZE

Now it's time to practice printing on paper. With your pencil, trace the dots and then practice on your own.

you you

Let's see if we can recognize the words in the picture below. Find the word 'you' in the word search below and circle the letters. Hint: The word is in the search 4 times.

c	k	y	o	u	d	y
g	d	x	m	y	u	o
d	l	q	z	o	g	u
y	o	u	d	u	w	

Amazing! You have finished all of the sight words.

ARE YOU HAVING FUN??

If you and your little ones have enjoyed the activities in this book, we would love it if you could leave us a quick review on Amazon. Reviews help other parents see if this book could be for them and are a great way for us to learn what you loved about our activities.

Even if it's just a few sentences, we read and appreciate them all!

ENJOY THE FOLLOWING BONUS PAGES TO ONE OF OUR NEW BOOKS!

'PRESCHOOL WRITING PAPER'

DON'T FORGET TO CUT OUT THE CRAFTS AT THE END!

Love always,
Emanuelle and Team

JUST FOR YOU

A FREE GIFT TO OUR READERS

Download a free sample of our next activity or coloring book and start enjoying all the fun new activities we send your way today! Visit this link:

www.teachmeforkids.com

TRACE THE LETTERS

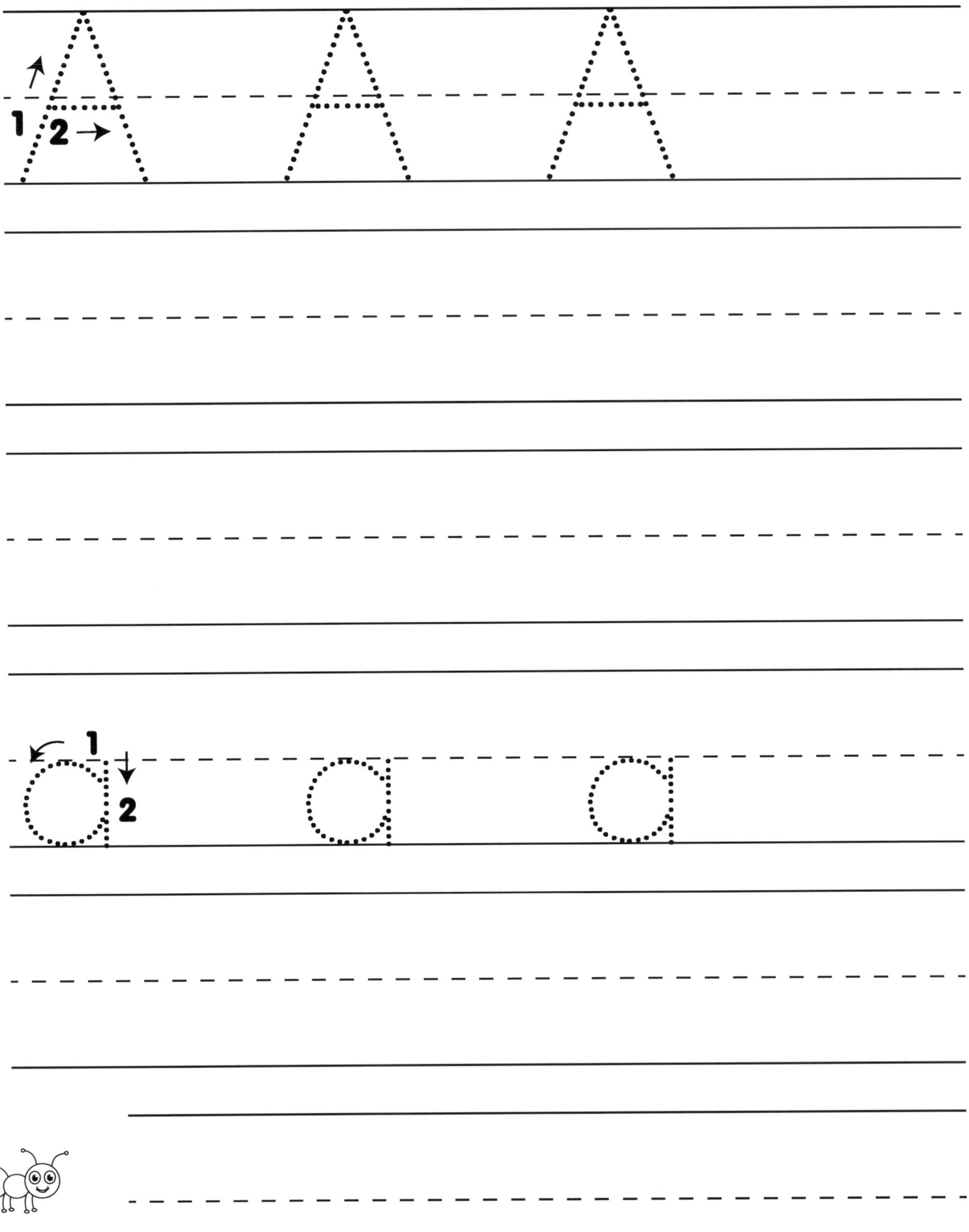

PRACTICE ON YOUR OWN

TRACE THE LETTERS

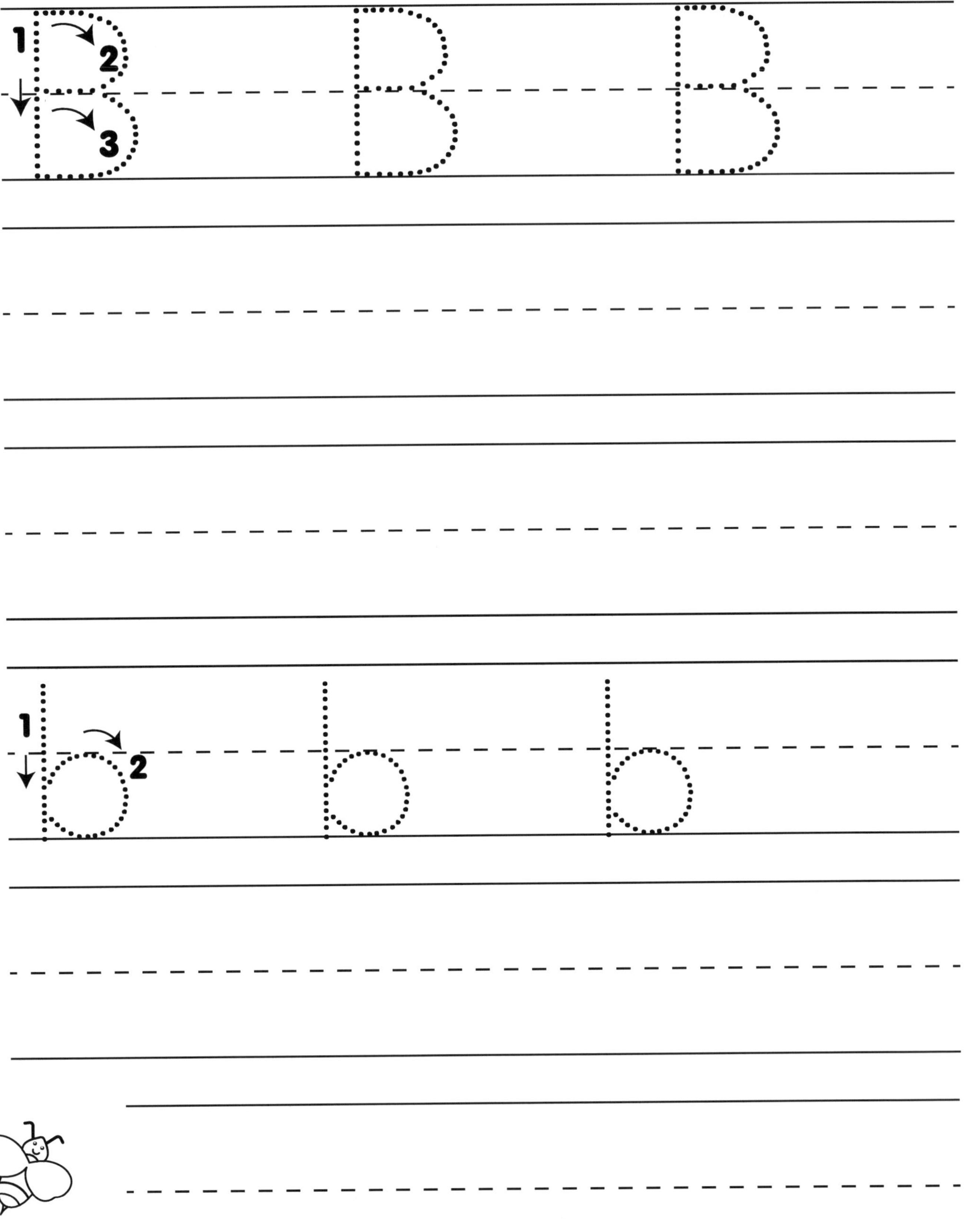

PRACTICE ON YOUR OWN

WRITE OUT ONE THING YOU LEARNED FROM YOUR BOOK

POPCORN CUT OUT CRAFT

Color in the popcorn kernels and the popcorn bag. Then practice writing your sightwords on the kernels. For every sightword you can print, you get to add that popcorn to your bag. See how much popcorn you can get in your bag!

CRAB CUT OUT CRAFT

Color the crab and all of his legs. Then cut out the pieces and glue the matching sightword legs onto his current legs.

THANK YOU FOR PRACTICING!

Made in the USA
Middletown, DE
16 November 2021